SEX DISCRIMINATION IN HIGHER EDUCATION

STRATEGIES FOR EQUALITY

Jennie Farley, editor

**NEW YORK STATE SCHOOL OF
INDUSTRIAL AND LABOR RELATIONS
CORNELL UNIVERSITY**

Cover design by Michael Rider

Library of Congress number: 81-9604
ISBN: 0-87546-089-5

Library of Congress Cataloging in Publication Data
Main entry under title:

Sex discrimination in higher education.

   Bibliography: p.
   Includes index.
   Based on papers presented at a conference held
in Nov. 1980 at Cornell University, sponsored by the
Extension and Public Service Division of the
School of Industrial and Labor Relations and other
organizations.
   1. Sex discrimination in education--United
States--Congresses. 2. Educational equalization--
United States--Congresses. 3. Education, Higher--
United States--Congresses. I. Farley, Jennie.
II. New York State School of Industrial and Labor
Relations. Extension and Public Service Division.
LC212.2.S485   378.73   81-9604
ISBN 0-87546-089-5 (pbk.)   AACR2

Copies may be ordered from

New York State School of
Industrial and Labor Relations
Cornell University
Ithaca, New York 14853

"Litigation represents a failure of creative approaches. (Effective mechanisms) for resolving disputes within institutions do not seem to exist yet but I do not think it is beyond our ingenuity to develop some...."
                              --Judith P. Vladeck

"The practice of true equal opportunity is patently less costly in terms of litigation, emotional damage, and other problems...."
                              --Mary P. Rowe

"It is clearly necessary to improve procedures and morality and thus the chance of justice being done...."
                              --Helen C. Davies and Robert E. Davies

"After ten years of affirmative action and federal legislation prohibiting sex discrimination, women are still second class citizens on the campus...but women are a new advocacy group--this is how we have to think of ourselves in the 1980s."
                              --Bernice R. Sandler

Contents

Preface

Jennie Farley

November 7-9, 1980, a conference on creative approaches
to ending sex discrimination in higher education drew one
hundred fifty-five--faculty members, academic administrators,
and attorneys--from two dozen colleges in ten states to
Cornell University. The theme was timely. That month, the
U.S. Department of Labor and the University of California
at Berkeley finally resolved a problem that had held up a
compliance review there for months. According to press
reports, the government agency and the university finally
compromised on the terms of granting access to personnel
documents and letters of reference for junior faculty being
considered for promotion. A University of Georgia professor
went to prison in his academic robes rather than respond to
a judicial order to tell how he had voted on the candidacy
for tenure of the director of women's studies there. And
the City University of New York, the State University of
New York, Notre Dame, Harvard, Princeton, and many other
institutions were defending themselves against law suits
and grievances alleging sex-based employment discrimination.
The week before the conference, Cornell itself was the tar-
get of a suit filed by a group known as the Cornell Eleven--
current and former faculty members who accused the institution of sex discrimination in hiring, contract renewal, promotion to tenure, and equity in pay.

Representatives of the institutions felt beleaguered
and drawn unwillingly into draining and expensive litigation.
Women grievants, reviewing the results of such court actions
in the past, were outraged that so few had succeeded, yet
determined to seek justice through the only avenue they saw
left to them. The issues are complex, but there seems to
be agreement on two premises: first, that there still is
sex discrimination in higher education and second, that law
suits are not effective mechanisms for resolving the problem.

Farley

Anthropologist Louise Lamphere and three other faculty
members brought a suit against Brown University charg-
ing sex discrimination in employment and lack of effective affirmative action. The case was certified as a
class action in July 1976. Fourteen months later, the
institution and the plaintiffs agreed to a court-super-
vised settlement, which involved the granting of tenure
to three of the four; the fourth, where tenure was not
at issue, received a financial settlement. Brown agreed
to change its policies but did not admit that it had been
guilty of sex discrimination. Both the plaintiffs and
the defendants in Lamphere et al. v. Brown University felt
that too much money had been spent on attorneys' fees.
The president of Brown, Howard Swearer, noted in the
February 1980 issue of the Brown Alumni Monthly that the
plaintiffs' attorneys' fees were twice as large as the
sums awarded to all the plaintiffs put together. "It
[the award to plaintiffs' attorneys] is equivalent to
the support of fifty financial aid students or fifteen
assistant professors," Swearer said. "It comes at a
time when most universities are hard-pressed financially."
    Despite that kind of agreement on the outcome of law
suits, there is comparatively little discussion of alternative ways of resolving the grievances of sex discrimination brought by women who say they have been victims of
it. Hence, the conference.
    The sponsor of this conference was the Extension and
Public Service Division of the New York State School of
Industrial and Labor Relations, Cornell, in cooperation
with three organizations: the Ithaca Branch of the
American Association of University Women; the Provost's
Advisory Committee on the Status of Women at Cornell; and
the Friends of the Cornell Eleven, an organization formed
to support the educational and legal efforts of the grievants. Twenty-one other campus and community groups supported the conference.[1] Partial financial support was
provided by the Ford Foundation and by the Aetna Life
and Casualty Foundation.
1. Cornell's Affirmative Action Advisory Board; Center for
Religion, Ethics, and Social Policy at Cornell; Cornell
Society of Women Engineers; Cornell University Panhellenic
Council; Cornell Women's Caucus; Cornell Women's Club of
Ithaca; Graduate School of Business and Public Administration Women's Association; Graduate Women in Science, Alpha
Chapter; Industrial and Labor Relations Women's Caucus; Men
Against Sexism and Rape; Minority Faculty/Staff Forum; Mortar
Board; Nothing But Treble; Noyes Center at Cornell; Profes-
sional Skills Roster; Tompkins County Human Rights Commission;

    As Dean Lois Gray, director of extension and public
service at the School of Industrial and Labor Relations,
noted in her welcoming remarks, the conference did not
represent a new departure for her unit. She said the
impetus for the school's founding had been the tragic
labor troubles in the United States. In 1944, to help
resolve those disputes, the New York legislature mandated
a new school--a place where pressing work problems could
be studied and taught about. They chose Cornell as the
site for the school because of the university's long
tradition as a land grant institution, a university that
puts special emphasis on extending the fruits of research
and teaching on campus to adults around the state.
    Since that time, men and women from all over the
world have come to the New York State School of Industrial
and Labor Relations at Cornell. People of both sexes, all
races, and all ages have participated in the extension programs offered on campus and across the state. Through
research reports and conference reports, the effects of
such extension are multiplied further. A president of
Cornell once introduced the graduates of the ILR school
at commencement as the "peacemakers of the world." In a
way, Dean Gray said, the two traditions came together in
the November 1980 conference. "We have always taken pride
in our efforts to be peacemakers and pride in Cornell's
record in extension and public service. Now in the 1980s,
we see a new kind of labor dispute--law suits resulting
from allegations of sex discrimination in higher education."
    The requirement that equal employment opportunity be
provided to academic women rests on two legal mandates:
Title VII of the Civil Rights Act of 1964 and Executive
Orders 11246 and 11375. The Civil Rights Act was amended
in 1972 to extend protection from discrimination on the
basis of sex to women professionals in higher education.
The executive orders, the first issued in 1965 and its
amendment in 1968, require that employers who do business
with the government not only not discriminate on the basis
of race, color, religion, sex, or national origin but that
they take "affirmative action" to ensure the provision of
equal opportunity, i.e., that they advertise widely, re-
examine their selection procedures to make certain women
are not being unfairly excluded, and so forth. Has this

Tompkins County National Organization for Women; Women's
Law Coalition; Women's Studies Program: Working Women's
Institute; and Zonta International.

legislation helped improve the status of academic women? At the very least, its existence has surely raised questions that were seldom raised in the past.

The conference speakers took quite different approaches to the resolution of problems created by sex discrimination in higher education. Attorney Judith Vladeck made it clear that if litigation in the courts is to be avoided, women who are victims of discrimination will have to be more aggressive in guarding their own rights; academic administrators will have to be more reasonable in dealing with grievances; and faculty members will have to be more open about their employment practices. Mary Rowe called on administrators and faculty to develop multiple helping resources for junior faculty and staff. Professors Helen and Robert Davies called for more honor among their colleagues and stressed the need for more objectivity in performance appraisals; they also emphasized the need for the development of sound and speedy grievance procedures. Activist Bernice Sandler urged women to organize in their own interests and to learn effective strategies for bringing about change in system-level policies and practices.

Before the conference, there was concern among the planners that few men's names appeared among the pre-registrants; indeed, as late as the week before the conference, only one man had signed up and paid his $15 registration fee--and he was one of the attorneys serving as counsel to women suing a university. A senior faculty woman wanted to come to the rescue. Faculty salaries are not keeping pace with inflation, she noted, and the fee might be a factor in keeping away tenured men. Therefore, she set up a scholarship fund for her male colleagues. The conference was so important, she said, that she did not want financial need to stand in the way of her male colleagues' attendance. Indeed, she said, she would not even require financial disclosure.

In the end, as can be seen from the list of participants (Appendix C), 14 percent of those who attended were men, none of whom was on scholarship. On a more serious note, there were undergraduate men among the participants. They were outnumbered, as were blacks and other minorities. But, as one participant observed, "This was the first conference I ever attended where minorities' concerns were linked with women's."

It is hoped that this book will be of use to diverse segments of the higher education community: faculty members

academic administrators, attorneys representing these
groups, and indeed, all those who care about both the
future of higher education and the welfare of individuals
within it. The volume includes not only the papers
presented at the conference but a summary of the discussion elicited by each presentation. The first chapter
of these proceedings is divided into three parts: a
review of the judicial history of academic women's
grievances written especially for this volume by attorney
Judith Vladeck; a transcript of Vladeck's presentation
at the conference; and a summary of the discussion that
followed. Chapter 2 is a report by Mary Rowe of MIT
(read in her absence by a Cornell faculty member) and
that discussion; Chapter 3 is the paper by professors
Helen and Robert Davies of the University of Pennsylvania
and the questions and answers that it elicited. Chapter
4 is the last paper presented that day--a call to action
presented by Bernice R. Sandler--and a summary of
that discussion. The concluding chapter contains reports
by conference participants of the progress and problems
at the colleges and universities they represented. Those
discussions suggested that, while these problems are sensitive and serious, there are creative ways of resolving
them where they should be resolved: on campus.

1.
Litigation: Strategy of the Last Resort

Judith P. Vladeck

JUDICIAL HISTORY

In 1972, Congress extended the coverage of Title VII to educational institutions, which had been exempted under the original act.[1] Despite the congressional mandate, however, between 1972 and 1977 the federal courts steadfastly refused to examine claims of discrimination in academic employment in the same manner in which they had dealt with claims of sex or race discrimination in industry. The difference in approach was rooted in the assumption, on the part of the judiciary, that a university was a "meritocracy," and that employment decisions made by institutions of higher education were not within the scope of judicial expertise. Therefore, it was concluded, university decisions were best left undisturbed. This attitude was made explicit by Judge Moore of the Second Circuit in Faro v. New York University:

> Of all fields which the federal
> courts should hesitate to invade

The research assistance of Paula Berg is gratefully acknowledged--J.P.V.

1. In the words of the House report on the amendment, "There is nothing in the legislative background of Title VII, nor does any national policy suggest itself to support the exemption of these educational institution employees--primarily teachers--from Title VII coverage. Discrimination against minorities and women in the field of education is as pervasive as in any other area of employment." H.R. Rep. No. 238, 92nd Cong., 2d Sess. (1971), reprinted in U.S. Code Cong. & Ad. News, 2137, 2155 (1972).

1

Vladeck

> and take over, education and faculty
> appointments at a university level
> are probably the least suited for fed-
> eral court supervision. Dr. Faro
> would remove any subjective judgments
> by her faculty colleagues in the deci-
> sion-making process by having the courts
> examine 'the university's recruitment,
> compensation, promotion and termination
> and by analyzing the way these procedures
> are applied to the claimant personally'....
> Such a procedure, in effect, would re-
> quire a faculty committee charged with
> recommending or withholding advancements
> or tenure appointments to subject itself
> to a court inquiry at the behest of un-
> successful and disgruntled candidates
> as to why the unsuccessful was not as
> well qualified as the successful.[2]

This hands-off attitude, exemplified by Judge Moore's
comments, placed a greater value on the sanctity of the
procedure used by universities in making employment
decisions than on safeguarding the right of minority
and woman employees to be evaluated without reference
to the irrelevancies of sex, race, or national origin.
Largely as a result of this attitude, virtually all
Title VII cases against universities in the period
between 1972 and 1977 ended in defeat for female
plaintiffs.

In the past two or three years, however, the federal judiciary has begun to retreat from its hands-off
policy. In fact, all circuit courts that have considered sex discrimination cases against academic
institutions have explicitly broken with this position.[3]

---

2. 502 F.2d 1229 (2d Cir. 1974) at 1231-32.

3. Between 1978 and 1980, the only circuit courts to
rule in academic discrimination cases, i.e., the First,
Second, Fifth and Seventh Circuits, expressly refused
to accept the deference shown to university employment
decision-making as spelled out in Faro v. New York University, supra. The reversal by these circuit courts
has been enunciated respectively in: Sweeney v. Board

2

It can also be argued that the Supreme Court has given
its tacit approval to the increased level of judicial
scrutiny of university employment practices, in that it
refused to grant review of a circuit court decision that
adopted this policy[4] and did not take issue with this aspect of a decision that it did review.[5]

The first court to reject the antiinterventionist
position was the Court of Appeals for the First Circuit
in the case of Sweeney v. Board of Trustees of Keene State
College. This case arose from the claim of discriminatory
refusal of the college to promote Sweeney to the level of
full professor, despite having awarded her tenure. Com-
menting on the record of the failure of plaintiffs in
Title VII cases to prevail against universities, Judge
Tuttle said,

> We voice misgivings over one theme re-
> current in those opinions: the notion
> that courts should keep 'hands-off'
> the salary, promotion, and hiring
> decisions of colleges and universities.
> This reluctance no doubt arises from
> the courts' recognition that hiring,
> promotion, and tenure decisions require
> subjective evaluation most appropriately
> made by persons thoroughly familiar with
> the academic setting. Nevertheless, we
> caution against permitting judicial def-
> erence to result in judicial abdication
> of a responsibility entrusted to the
> courts by Congress. That responsibility
> is simply to provide a forum for the

---

of Trustees of Keene State College, 569 F.2d (1st Cir.
1978); 439 U.S. 24, 58 L.Ed. 2d 216, 99 S.Ct. 295 (1978);
remanded, 604 F.2d 106 (1st Cir. 1979); Jepsen v. Florida
Board of Regents, 610 F.2d 1379 (5th Cir. 1980); Powell v.
Syracuse University, 580 F.2d 1150 (2d Cir. 1978), cert.
denied 439 U.S. 984, 58 L.Ed.2d 656, 99 S.Ct. 576 (1978);
Davis v. Weidner, 596 F.2d (7th Cir. 1979).

4. Powell v. Syracuse University, supra.

5. Sweeney v. Board of Trustees of Keene State College,
supra.

> litigation of complaints of sex
> discrimination in institutions of
> higher learning as readily as for
> other Title VII suits.[6]

The court found in favor of Sweeney, ordered that the
college promote her, and awarded back pay.

Six months later, the Court of Appeals for the
Second Circuit, the court that had articulated the
hands-off policy in Faro in 1974, reversed its position.
In Powell v. Syracuse University, a black female, who
was a visiting professor of architecture, brought a
Title VII action against the university for failing to
hire her as a full-time faculty member. While the
court ruled against Powell, it took the opportunity
to announce that it had reconsidered its position in
Faro and would henceforth subject the employment practices of universities to an increased level of scrutiny.
It described the role of the courts in academic discrimination cases:

> It is our task, then, to steer a
> careful course between excessive
> intervention in the affairs of the
> university and the unwarranted
> tolerance of unlawful behavior.
> Faro does not, and was never intended
> to, indicate that academic freedom
> embraces the freedom to discriminate.[7]

With the change in approach has come a willingness to
impose remedies that the courts had previously refused to
consider. In Kunda v. Muhlenberg College, a female physical
education instructor brought a Title VII suit for failure to
promote and award tenure. After finding that "discriminatory
animus based on sex" motivated the failure of the dean and
president of the college to tell Kunda that a master's degree
was an absolute prerequisite to advancement, the court ordered
that "...she be awarded tenure contingent upon obtaining her
Master's degree within two full school years."[8] While Kunda's

---

6. 569 F.2d 176-77 (1st Cir. 1978), supra.

7. 580 F.2d 1154 (2d Cir. 1978), supra.

8. Kunda v. Muhlenberg College, 463 F.Supp. 294, 308 (E.D.
Pa. 1978). Despite the fact that the plaintiff did not have

4

case was unusually strong, her case marks the first time
that a court, upon finding that sex discrimination tainted
a university's decision to grant or withhold tenure, has
substituted its evaluation of a faculty member for that
of the university.

The opening of the court doors to plaintiffs who
bring sex discrimination actions against universities is
a step forward in the effort to achieve the goals of Title
VII. This is not to say, however, that plaintiffs face an
easy task in proving, by a preponderance of the evidence,
that "discriminatory animus based on sex" biased a university's employment decision.[9] There has been a wide
disparity in the willingness of courts to probe beneath
the subjective rationalizations offered by defendants in
rebuttal to a plaintiff's prima facie case of disparate
treatment.[10] Some courts also continue to demonstrate

---

a master's degree, her colleagues in the department of
physical education and other departments in the college,
recommended that she be awarded tenure.

9. Since 1978, only three academic discrimination suits
have resulted in final judgments favorable to the plaintiff: Sweeney v. Board of Trustees of Keene State
College, supra; Kunda v. Muhlenberg College, supra;
Jepsen v. Florida Board of Regents, supra. On the losing
side, Powell v. Syracuse University, supra; Smith v. University of North Carolina, 18 FEP Cases 913 (M.D.N.C.
1978); Cooper v. University of Texas at Dallas, 482 F.Supp.
187 (N.D. Tex. 1979); Davis v. Weidner, supra; Lieberman
v. Gant, 474 F.Supp. 848 (D. Conn. 1979); Campbell v.
Ramsay, 484 F.Supp. 190 (E.D. Ark. 1980).

10. For example, in Sweeney v. Board of Trustees of
Keene State College, supra, at 179, the court did not
accept as sufficient, the defendant's blanket assertion
that, in "their honest belief," the plaintiff was simply
less qualified for the promotion than the selected male
candidate. In contradistinction to this, some courts
have demonstrated a complete willingness to accept an
employer's "good faith" assessment of a plaintiff's
qualifications as sufficient to meet its burden. For
example, in Lieberman v. Gant, supra, at 865, the court
said that "...a sincere belief that a person is not
qualified for a job is an adequate justification for
an employment decision and rebuts a complainant's prima
facie case."

Vladeck

a lack of sensitivity to the more subtle aspects of sex
discrimination in the academic setting.[11] Nevertheless,
the promise of the courts to scrutinize the employment
practices of universities, as it would those of any other
employer, signifies the falling of a significant barrier
to the realization of employment equality in academia.

ONE LITIGATOR'S EXPERIENCE

I understand my presentation is to summarize the ways
in which the law protects academic women. That is easy:
it does not. The theme today is creativity in dealing
with problems of sex discrimination in academic employment
and the search for alternatives to litigation. Those of
us who are lawyers think of litigation as failure, failure
of the creative efforts to solve problems. Had there been
creativity, there would have been no need for litigation.
On the other hand, I know, as yet, of no alternative to it.

Since the early 1970s, I have been involved in litigation in one forum or another against universities. My
first involvement was not only on behalf of women, but
also on behalf of unions, when unions first began to organize college faculties. I learned that most administrative
agencies and most courts really do not understand the university or its employment practices. An administrative law

---

11. The "old boy" method of recruiting and hiring faculty
members, while seemingly innocent enough, has actually
been one efficient means whereby women (not part of the
network) have been systematically excluded from academic
job opportunities. See Vladeck and Young, Sex Discrimination in Higher Education: It's Not Academic, 2 Women's
Rights L. Rep. 59 (1978). Some judges have failed to
acknowledge the effect of the network in perpetuating
exclusionary practices. This blindness appears in a Title
VII action against an elementary school for failing to
hire the plaintiff as a teacher. In Lombard v. School
District of the City of Erie, 463 F.Supp. 566, 571 (W.D.
Pa. 1978), the court noted, "Stating that a man was
selected over a woman for a job because the man had more
friends in high places, constitutes a 'non-discriminatory
reason' for unequal treatment sufficient to avoid liability
under Title VII...."

6

judge or a judge in a district court is baffled by the
language. The terminology—the deans, and the provosts,
and the adjuncts, and the tenure track—is such mystical
language that it creates a problem for the ordinary judge
trying to understand the employment practices of universities. This has caused a certain hands-off policy. If
they don't understand it, they want to leave it alone.

Not only in the union cases, but later in the discrimination cases, the same kind of bafflement has arisen
from the mystique of the university. But the mystique is
perpetuated by both sides: I was once soundly chastised
by my own clients for calling university faculty members
"employees." That is not a proper word to use, I learned,
for people who work for universities. They are not
employees. They are something else.

About 1971, a group of women from the City University
of New York came to see me. They had filed charges with
HEW and were considering filing a class action suit on
behalf of the CUNY women faculty and other women professional employees. They asked if I would represent them.
I said I wished they would find a younger lawyer. I felt
I was too late for the revolution, but because there were
no other lawyers who had sufficient experience and willingness to represent them, I agreed to, and I became, at my
age, a "cause" lawyer. I didn't start out as one, but
this decade of experience has radicalized me. I am now likely
to exhort women grievants, that is, women and members of
minority groups employed in the academic environment, to
fight for treatment equal to that provided to their white
male colleagues.

There is discrimination in the university against anyone who is not a white Anglo Saxon male. Women and members
of minority groups are likely to be judged not on merit but
on other factors totally unrelated to the standards that
are alleged to be used in assessing the performance of
faculty members. I am currently counsel to plaintiffs in
two major class action suits against academic institutions:
one against the City University of New York on behalf of
all its female professional employees and the other against
the State University of New York at Stony Brook on behalf
of all its female professionals, both faculty and nonteach-
ing professionals. I have successfully settled a class
action against the Polytechnic Institute of New York.

Each of these cases was preceded by lengthy efforts on
the part of the plaintiffs to get some kind of remedy within

7

the institution without having to bring suit. The
experiences of the women at CUNY are instructive. They
had gathered data showing clearly that women's salaries
were different from men's, their rate of hire was different, the level of position at the time of hire was
different, and their rates of earning tenure and promotion were different. The women organized into a political caucus, went to the chancellor, and said, "We do not
want to sue on these issues. We don't want to fight.
We just want somebody to look at this and straighten it
out." The chancellor's response was a fiasco, as a
political gesture. In setting up a committee to study
this situation, he bypassed the women who had come to
him originally and appointed a group of strangers--
women who had no prior identification with women's issues.
He alienated the grievants; they said, "Let's not trust
those women appointed by the chancellor." The chancellor
remained aloof, but his commission went ahead and prepared
a report that concluded, "Discrimination against women is
pervasive throughout the university." Whereupon, the
women, who had originally complained, seized upon the report
as their very own, while the chancellor said, "One cannot
rely on this report; the statistics are not reliable, and
so on."

A similar situation occurred at SUNY. The women there
had the NOW chapter of Suffolk County and other women's
organizations that begged the university to do something.
Other supporters, women statisticians, women sociologists,
and other experts who were familiar with the kinds of
studies that should be performed to determine whether or
not discrimination exists, had urged that a study be made.
They themselves did what they called a "salary equity study,"
and there again the president repudiated the study and said
he was going to do his own. Sometime afterward, where the
administration found salary differentials that were "too
extreme," the administration "corrected" them. But the
administration would not report to the women as to how it
determined whose salary should be raised or on what basis
it was making these decisions, and the women were angered
enough to find a lawyer.

There is almost a pattern of women making heroic
efforts to try to resolve the problems within the establishment and being forced, through total frustration, to
seek other avenues. The blindness of universities in
those situations is something I do not understand. Perhaps

there is some master plan in which somebody thinks about it and says, "It is cheaper for us to wait the five or seven years that the litigation will take than to undertake a voluntary study now."

I cannot believe the indifference. After six or seven years of litigation against CUNY, we went to trial in June on only the salary issue. In May, the university said to the court, "We need more time to look into the issue, to do a study to see whether or not there is salary discrimination." I was in such a rage that I said, "How dare a government institution, which was charged with discrimination six or seven years ago, not have looked into this, not have studied it, not have done anything to determine whether these allegations were true or false?" The judge was not persuaded by the university either. We went to trial and are awaiting a decision.

The form that a class action suit takes—and I think the Cornell Eleven is probably typical of the actions women have taken—is that one or two or eleven brave people stand up and say, "We believe that our experiences—ones in which we have suffered discriminatory treatment—are characteristic of the experiences being had by other people like us." If the court is persuaded that these women are representative of the group they purport to speak for, the court will then appoint those individuals as class representatives. Thereafter, the case can proceed with those representatives acting as spokespersons for the class. The class is defined by the court and generally will include all women who are "similarly situated."

To try to prove sex discrimination in an individual case is a doomed effort. There is not a single one of us who cannot be destroyed. Once woman stands up and says, "I am as good as they are. And they are promoted and I wasn't." There is almost no way you can prevail in that situation. The institution is going to bring out twenty witnesses who represent a gathering of forces to say that the plaintiff is disgruntled, less scholarly, or otherwise less deserving than her so-called peers. The individual, the outsider, is going to be defeated.

The class action device is necessary to avoid being sidetracked by discussion of individual merit. If one can show a pattern of discrimination against women (or blacks, or older people), then the presumption is that the individual employment decisions affecting a member of the protected class are tainted by the same discrimination that disadvantages the class.

The characteristic form of these cases is that they proceed with an effort to show a pattern; this pattern is typically established with statistics. Because it is very difficult and time-consuming to make a case by bringing in thousands of individual cases, a procedure has been developed by which we show statistical patterns. It was easy in the early days of the civil rights cases in the South to show that the work force was all white at the top and all black at the bottom. In some cases, I have used charts to show the same distribution of males and females; that at the upper levels, there are no women at all. Zero. It is useful to use some visual aids, charts or graphs, to show the court the pattern against which the individual cases can be viewed. It is fascinating to see where women are located in the pyramid.

The class action has become a battle of statistics. I can demonstrate very easily that the women are here and the men are all over there. Then the university says, "The numbers are correct--we can't argue with them. But there is an explanation." That is when we get into the battle of the heavyweights. At SUNY, we are seeing an example of this. The plaintiffs have a fine statistician whose report demonstrated that there was discrimination against all women. There was a salary spread that was unexplained when the women were matched against the men in terms of the time of receipt of Ph.D. degree, the quality of the institution from which they had graduated, and most of the other classic indicators that are used to compare academics' qualifications. But the state university brought in an expert and then another expert and then a third expert, trying to explain why women are where they are. I feel certain that the court is going to be absolutely dazzled by all of the numbers and theories of labor economists who say that the differential between male and female salaries can be explained in terms of "human capital." (I recommend to you that, if you are interested in these matters, you familiarize yourself with the jargon. That is essential to understanding these arguments.) The human capital theory holds that we are what we invest in ourselves; thus it can be expected that because women interrupt their work more often than men, women are less productive. Generally, since very few absolute measures of productivity can be identified in academic employment, the defense has begun to use

other surrogate measures. I am satisfied that there is
no valid explanation of the salary difference other than
discrimination.

What I am concerned about is that the court is
likely to be baffled by the numbers as well as by the
obfuscations offered by the university. Judges seem to
be perfectly willing to accept almost any explanation
that allows them to avoid involving themselves in the
sacred academic process. This is why it is essential
that, in addition to the statistics, we present cases
of individuals who actually have experienced discrimination so that the court can understand how these practices
operate and how they affect living, breathing human beings.
Numbers are not enough.

I used a statistical witness in one case, and the
judge, a very literate man, said, "I refuse to rely on
the regressive analysis that was presented by plaintiff's
expert." The judge was so literate that I am convinced
the word regressive was deliberately chosen. We cannot
rely on statistics alone. We must rely on the kinds of
testimony that will give the court an understanding of
how the system really works, that is, how the committees
work, how there are departments that still say, "We don't
want women," and how the committees work when there is
fighting over promotions or tenure.

When we get to that point in the testimony, we run
into the university's defense that any discussions at
the committee level are confidential and privileged.
Should the university be permitted to stonewall with a
statement that discussions concerning personnel decision-
making are confidential? Should it be permitted to say
it is not going to have testimony with regard to that, so
it isn't going to turn over files, or that it isn't going
to permit access to personnel files even though courts
have permitted access to this information in every other
kind of employment discrimination case?

When a case involves university employment, somehow
the judges think, "Well, that's not nice." The courts
have imposed the most elaborate system of coding so that
we can't tell whose file we are looking at. The professor
in Georgia went to jail to make this point, that universities are sacred cows, that their personnel decision-making
is somehow uniquely protected. That isn't so. Without
access to the information about what went on behind closed
doors, we can't enforce Title VII.

11

Vladeck

Another problem of litigating these cases, other
than the massive resistance of the universities and
their digging in their heels, is that delay is the
classic defense of university lawyers. But more
importantly, there is another problem, women and minorities who are suffering from discrimination themselves
resist organizing to do anything about it. I am sure
that the Cornell Eleven, like the CUNY Twenty-Six and
the SUNY Twenty-One, are treated like pariahs in many
parts of the university system. They are the great
unwashed, and they are not supported. Women who have
made it up to the level of department chairperson and
to other positions of influence and power somehow resist
the idea of supporting the women who have not. There
is an elitism that seems to affect these people who are
secure and who have reached positions of comfort and
security: They are there because of merit. The others
who haven't gotten there? They're just not that good.
It is a pervasive attitude among women and among blacks
who have moved up into positions of supervision, and it
is a serious obstacle.

There is also a kind of dishonesty pervading the
universities' approach to these problems. An example I
can offer occurred in the preparation of one witness who
was going to testify about a college committee (other
than his own) that was searching for candidates and
wouldn't accept applications from women. He was upset
about it. After he left, I went over the records of his
own department, where he had served on the personnel
committee in his department, and found there had never
been a woman full professor, although his discipline is
in the social sciences in a field studded with competent
women. There is absolutely no satisfactory explanation
for the fact that there had never been a woman full
professor. So I am not moved by his righteous indignation
about other departments when his own seems to be an
offender. But this kind of blindness pales in comparison
to the rationalizations offered by the administrators.

Why do we bring these lawsuits at all, when they
cost so much money, they hurt so much, and they get
such questionable results? The answers are these: there
is nothing else we can do, and by bringing these lawsuits,
we do have considerable effect on universities. If nothing
else, we have pushed them to improve the writing of the advertisements for job openings and to improve their record

keeping. I have seen a ripple effect. You will find that, if you do your own statistical analysis of the situation here at Cornell, women who are entering now are getting a better shake than those who entered ten years ago or fifteen years ago. Now women who are entitled to be brought in as assistant professors are not being brought in as lecturers while their male counterparts automatically get assistant professorships. I think we have raised their consciousness. Those authorities who review the hiring decisions are worried. Now they don't write an ad that describes only one living human being--one living white male.

With the new self-consciousness and with the bringing in of women at the appropriate level, there is an educational process that goes forward. Men in the chemistry department who never had to work with a woman before now know that the women aren't going to go tripping off, leaving their test tubes, to take care of their babies in six months, leaving the men in terrible straits. Perhaps as women are being hired in places where they have never been before, women will be moving up into the tenured associate professorships and professorships. But I know of no process other than litigating unfair decisions now open to us.

If you are capable, in your department or in your college, of getting what you want and deserve and still avoiding litigation, of course you should. Bringing suit is terribly expensive and draining, but if there is no other course and it is long past time when the university should bring about voluntary change, then litigation is your only alternative. The people who are brave enough to be among the one or two or three out there speaking for all are people who deserve your support, your help, and your assistance. They are fighting a very important battle. I congratulate the Cornell Eleven and all who have made this conference possible.

DISCUSSION

Women Administrators. One participant rose to the defense of the few women administrators who have made their way up through the system, and then, seemingly, won't reach down to help junior women. "Although they may not appear to be helpful," she said, "we have to be understanding. They may be under great pressure themselves." Another participant commented that women administrators in the SUNY system who choose to challenge the system, for example, on the issue of salaries, are not only taking on their own administration but they are challenging the governor's division of the budget. "It's my perception," she said, "that even the staff in the office of the chancellor of SUNY would be hesitant to do anything sweeping about redressing wrongs because they would need authorization from the people who control the state budget." Women administrators and others are having to operate under guidelines handed down from that level, she said.

To the first, Vladeck said that might indeed be the case, but there is a time to stand up and be counted. That time is when junior women grievants need support from senior women.

To the second, Vladeck said, "The administrators at CUNY also are operating under considerable financial pressure. We have finished the trial on the salary issue there. We are attempting to demonstrate that there is something like a six million dollar difference per year in female and male salaries that can be explained only by discriminatory low salaries paid to females. When we concluded the presentations on both sides, the judge invited both of us into chambers. 'I still think,' he said, 'that you ought to settle this.' The woman representing City University said, 'Indeed not, Your Honor. We couldn't think of it.' The judge responded, 'If I find against you , you have enormous liability. Have you conveyed this to your principals?' 'I cannot conceive of losing,' she answered. The judge said, 'Suppose that you do.' 'We'll appeal at once,' she said. To which the judge said, 'And after you have been to the World Court, what will you do then?'

"The fact is that, very often, government entities, after rational consideration of alternatives, do settle a monetary claim. Surely the chancellor of a state university or a city university has access to money for equity adjustments. Equity adjustments are all that is required to avoid what can potentially be enormous back pay liability. Presented this way, I see no reason why a considered judgment to settle cannot be made."

Awkward Position of Lawyers. A participant observed that attorneys are in a difficult position because they have to prepare two cases at once: first, the statistical argument

14

and second, the personal cases. Vladeck said that was
precisely the problem--that, plus the hostile judiciary.
These are the hardest cases, she said, and nobody but
dedicated people would take them on. The documentary
evidence is in the hands of the opposition. In order to
make your case, you have to get access to the records,
which are jealously guarded by the defendant. Another
problem is that the defendants are frightened people.
"In the one individual case which I won in New York State,
I went into the appellate division, which is the second
level of court, with a defendant who had been denied promotion on the grounds that she was 'pushy' since she had
asked to be considered for promotion. She lost in the
lower court and, in the appellate division, she was faced
by five prominent judges. One of them leaned over to
another and said, 'What was she complaining about, anyway?
She had a job--and jobs in the academic world are hard to
get, I understand.' I was so infuriated that I threw out
my arms and said, 'It is going to take two generations of
change on this bench before any woman will get a fair
hearing.' They didn't wait until I was out of the courtroom before they affirmed the decision of the lower court.
One of my proudest moments came when the Court of Appeals
reversed them unanimously, saying that people who fight
for their rights are often deemed to be troublemakers but
that the law does not require that people be supine."

Settlement out of Court. One participant asked the speaker
what advice she had for plaintiffs in class actions who
were offered settlement out of court. "Settlement is
almost always preferable to extended litigation," Vladeck
said. "If one is bringing a class action, the remedy sought
is not just money, it is changes in practices and procedures
as well. If you settle, even for less than everything you
want, you get those changes into the system faster."
    For individual cases, Vladeck said, the decision
whether or not to settle has to be made by the individual
woman herself. The effects of exhaustion are usually felt
much more severely by the plaintiff than by the institution.
The plaintiff is without resources, perhaps low on stamina.
The damage to the plaintiff's psyche cannot be ignored. "I
have seen women absolutely devastated by the experience of
having their ability as researchers or as teachers attacked.
They really know that they are good, but then to have their
colleagues say, 'Her scholarship was marginal' is a terrible
blow.

"Sometimes they say, 'We didn't want to give her tenure because somebody better might come along.' I call that the Doctrine of the Second Coming. The damage to the individual is something you really have to appraise. If it is somebody young, tough, and strong, well, she may be able to go the whole route."

Remarking that that kind of devastation is usually suffered by individuals alone, one participant asked, "Is there any effort to get these women in different departments on different campuses together so that they can help one another bear these sickening disappointments and make these hard decisions?" Vladeck responded that she thought that was one of the purposes of the conference.

"Perhaps we remember our losses better than our wins," Vladeck suggested in response to another question about helping male faculty to accept women as colleagues. She was representing a woman at Staten Island Community College who was claiming that she had not been promoted for discriminatory reasons. A tenured full professor who had sat on one of the committees reviewing her case turned to her and said, "If I could testify on your behalf I would like to do so. The discussion which went on about your candidacy was not what I would call academic judgment." That case was arbitrated--there was a union contract that provided for arbitration--and Vladeck helped prepare the professor for his participation in the hearings. During those discussions, the professor said, "I am not going to testify unless I am ordered to do so by the arbitrator," and explained that his institution has a rule of confidentiality. So Vladeck said to the arbitrator, "Direct the professor to respond." The arbitrator asked the attorney for the college, who said, "Indeed there is such a rule and we enforce it. We bring people up on charges of 'conduct unbecoming a faculty member' if they violate that rule." "I asked the institution to waive the rule of confidentiality so that the professor could testify. The college refused to testify and the arbitrator refused to direct him to violate the rule of confidentiality. We went to the Court of Appeals on that one. The court ruled that when there is a union contract that does not expressly require otherwise, all rules of the institution must be observed. There is no guarantee of due process in arbitration. Even though the rule of confidentiality was upheld in state court,

I don't believe that the rule will stand in federal
court," Vladeck said.

Dangers Ahead. In response to a question, Vladeck said
she did foresee some losses because of the new Reagan
administration. "I don't see any great loss to women and
minorities if we lose the Equal Employment Opportunity
Commission and all the state administrative agencies. The
one thing Governor Reagan had going for him was that these
agencies were a great waste of money. The EEOC has done
virtually nothing; it certainly hasn't come into this area
at all. HEW has been absolutely useless in the last decade
since they've had jurisdiction over this area. And the
state division? I am sure you all have terrible stories
to exchange. They can wipe out the state administrative
agencies, as far as I am concerned. What does worry me is
that the lower court judges, who have enormous power, the
district court judges, anticipating the change in the
Supreme Court and anticipating the change in the circuit
courts, wanting to make their decisions 'on the right
side,' so they won't be reversed, may well be more cautious.
On the other hand, they can't be much more cautious than
they have been in this area. So we can't lose too much.

Brown Case and University of Minnesota Case. [For a summary
of the Brown case, see Preface. At the University of Minnesota, chemist Shyamala Rajender was denied a tenure-
track post in 1973. She filed a sex discrimination suit
that was later certified as a class action. In 1980, after
eleven weeks of trial, the court awarded Rajender $100,000;
in addition, a quota was imposed on the chemistry department
and a "special master" was appointed by the court. That
person is to resolve all past or future sex discrimination
claims, to award cash damages or faculty positions, including tenure, and to oversee hiring at the university until
1989.] Why were these cases so successful? Vladeck opined
that in the Minnesota case (1) there is a federal district
court judge in the Minnesota area who is both liberal and
intelligent and (2) the institution is comparatively small
so that it was easy to demonstrate male-female differences
in status and rank.

"As for Brown," she said, "there are lots of stories
about why the university settled. There are rumors. But
one explanation is that there were documents and other
kinds of evidence that the university did not want to have

17

made public. I do not know the full story, but
I do know that the settlement has not yet been fully
implemented, so that it is still in litigation. Incidentally, these are not spectacular cases. What will be
spectacular is when a major university agrees to voluntarily change its practices and procedures."

The CUNY Case. "At the City University of New York,"
Vladeck said, "there is a substantial pay gap between the
men's average salary and the women's average salary. That
is acknowledged by all. But when the university set out
to prepare its defense, it sent out a questionnaire. The
questionnaire had some two hundred questions of which some
were not objectionable: Where did you do graduate work?
What year did you complete your degree? What year were
you hired here? What prior experience did you have?
What research have you undertaken? How many books have
you published? Research articles? Nobody could quarrel
with that.
    "The next set of questions dealt with family. What
are the ages of your children? What is your spouse's occupa-
tion? If your spouse had a job offer in another place,
would you be willing to relocate? Then there were questions
(literally) asking what time the respondents get up in the
morning and what time they go to bed. How much time do you
spend in household chores? In child care? In meditation,
encounter therapy, and--I think--yoga? I thought this was
an outrageous invasion of privacy.
    "When I saw the copy of that questionnaire, I went to
the judge and said, 'You can't let this happen.' The judge
asked the city, 'What is this all about? Why are you asking these questions?' They believed that the answers to
these questions would help them to demonstrate that there
is a difference in productivity between males and females,
and the judge, not understanding this, said, 'Well, they are
your employees, you can ask them anything you want to.' The
women did not rise up in a body in protest against this
questionnaire. I couldn't say to them what I wanted to say:
'Idiots! Don't answer those questions.' Many men did not
answer them, but ironically, great numbers of the women did.
The response required a signature, and although it was not
obligatory, the cover letters describing it as "voluntary
cooperation" with the researchers collecting data for the
forthcoming litigation were so unclear that many women
claimed not to have understood them.

"Vast numbers of women responded to these questions, spelling out meticulously the 2.3 hours they spend in, let's say, encounter therapy each week. Men turned out to be more resistant to these questions. Most interesting of all, the results were such that the statisticians couldn't use them, so absolutely inconclusive that they had no meaning. They had all these data, and they couldn't extract anything meaningful from them. There didn't seem to be any significant differences between the men and the women in any of the variables."

Alternate Forums. In response to a question, Vladeck said she would like to see alternate channels for the resolution of grievances because she feels that the court is not the appropriate forum for resolving an individual case. But she didn't believe that the forums developed under union contracts are appropriate. She based this, she said, on her limited experience. "I don't believe that most arbitrators, who are not required to be lawyers, are qualified. I also believe that arbitrators who regularly deal with the university are not likely to be sympathetic to the woman or the black who says, 'This institution has mistreated me.' Arbitrators begin to develop an identification with the establishment," Vladeck held.

"I believe," Vladeck said, "that there are modifications of the classic labor arbitration that could be developed for use in these cases. What I would like to do is to first reach agreement that there is a problem and then bring in, with the agreement of both sides, a neutral. If the grievant is a woman, then she doesn't have to begin at ground zero, setting out to prove that there is discrimination against women at her institution. While I am not aware of any such mechanisms operating effectively at present, I do not think it is beyond our ingenuity to develop some."

Internal Appellate Procedures. "Supposing you were advising the university instead of the grievants," one participant asked, "what kind of internal appellate procedures would you advise them to set up?" Vladeck answered that there should be designees of the university and designees of the grievants serving as an appellate body. There should be a final step, a neutral. It would almost be the old tripartite arbitration system, but in two steps.

19

The appellate body then has control outside that of the jurisdiction of either of the contending parties.

In setting up that system, Vladeck said, there has to be consultation with potential grievants and with the administration of a university. It is an adversary procedure. You have to have agreement on both sides that, if they cannot themselves dispose of the issue, there is some outside neutral party on whom they will rely and whose decisions will bind them.

This is tricky because within the university it is the conviction that departments decide who they want to hire and promote. But at City University, Vladeck noted, there has been formed what is called under the collective bargaining agreement the Select Faculty Committee representing both sides; that committee in turn has the power to select a third party.

If the institution is not willing to cede enough sovereignty to a neutral to resolve these disputes, then, Vladeck asserted, they must go to court. As a compromise, then, the two sides can decide on their neutral so that they are not dependent on the whim of a judge in their district. They can choose somebody who has familiarity with academic procedures and academic establishments. This requires, of course, that the university concede that somebody outside itself might be superior to it. That concession may prove to be the insurmountable obstacle.

A faculty member asked how neutrals are selected. Vladeck noted that a neutral does not necessarily have to have had no prior association with the employing institution. "I could conceive of a professor or a former administrator of the university being a neutral," she added. "What you look for in a neutral is the quality of honesty, the willingness to listen to the testimony, and the ability to make an even-handed decision. Find the local rabbi, the priest, or the retired provost," she suggested. "You would be satisfied that they are people above reproach whose probity you would not question."

Grievances. A participant asked if an institution is covered by a union contract, could a grievant use both the union grievance procedure and the EEOC procedures? Suppose an arbitrator rules that there has been no discrimination, can the grievant still take her case outside?

The answer, Vladeck said, is yes: "You are not bound by the decision of an arbitrator or to any decision reached

by the state human rights division or the EEOC. Even if
these agencies decide there is no probable cause to
believe that sex discrimination has taken place, you can
still go into federal court. There is a Supreme Court
decision to that effect, Alexander v. Gardner Denver,
which says that the federal court has plenary power; it
will not be barred from looking at any decision reached
through arbitration. That was the case of a black man
who claimed race discrimination. He had lost in arbitration, and the EEOC had bowed to the arbitrator's decision.
The Court said, 'We might look at what the arbitrator
decided, but we will not be bound by it.'

"The practical result is that, if you are undertaking
a union grievance, you will find that it will proceed
slowly. If you are going to meet the time requirements,
which is now 240 days for filing with the EEOC, the chance
of your having a resolution of your grievance through the
union grievance procedure is limited. There are contracts
which say that if a grievant goes to EEOC, you may not
arbitrate; employers are saying, "Why should we have to
litigate on two fronts." Some women have lost because
they believed that they could go through arbitration and
then, if they had received no satisfaction there, they
could still go to the EEOC. But they have sometimes
discovered that, by the time they got to the EEOC, they
were time-barred.

"There is another consideration: this is exhausting
work. You may not want to do it unless you have confi-
dence in the first forum, which may serve as a rehearsal
for what you can expect the next time around. But I
cannot imagine a grievant voluntarily doing it more than
once."

It was noted by a member of the audience that, if
one goes through a union grievance procedure, the union
ordinarily pays the lawyers' fees. But, she noted, "we
have no sex discrimination clause in our grievance procedures." Could there be a clause in a contract, she
asked, that protected both the grievant's right to arbitration on sex discrimination and also her right, should
that fail, to file with the EEOC? Vladeck allowed as
how there could be such a clause and composed one handily:
"The arbitration provision shall include any claim of
discrimination based on race, color, religion, or sex.
In the event that the grievant who alleges such discrimination files with a government agency, the arbitration

21

Vladeck

process may still be invoked; but filing to preserve
timeliness with a government agency shall not influence
the arbitration process."

2.

Building Mentorship Frameworks as Part of an Effective Equal Opportunity Ecology

Mary P. Rowe

Educational institutions, government agencies, corporations, and other organizations can help build mentoring frameworks for women and men. This paper discusses five major points in building institutional devices that help women find the multiple sources of help which many people think of as mentorship and which are now seen by many people to be indispensable for career success.[1]

Each of these points may be seen as necessary, but not sufficient by itself, to establish the supportive ecology in which excellent mentorship is available to women (and men). My own view is that the barriers to adequate mentorship for women are sufficiently high that a successful framework requires energy from many sources: creative support of top management, women's networks, close relation between top management and the networks, receptive individuals seeking helping resources, and specific programs tailored to each kind of worker in each kind of organization. Each of these energy sources

---

Mary Rowe could not be present at the conference. Her paper was read for her by June Fessenden-Raden of Cornell; discussion afterwards was led by Fessenden-Raden and Bernice R. Sandler.

1. In this paper, I use mentor in its widest possible meaning to refer to coaching, guidance, sponsorship in the context set forth by Garrison and Davis, master's thesis, MIT Sloan School, 1979, and by Shapiro, Haseltine, and Rowe in Sloan Management Review, spring 1978.

Rowe

has its own role to play; all are needed for an effective equal opportunity ecology.[2]

LEGITIMATION AS WELL AS LEADERSHIP

Whatever the institution or agency or corporation, the top administration must announce and then exemplify commitment to equal opportunity. In formal and informal situations top management must be seen to have a coherent, consistent policy. This policy should appear frequently: in annual reports, in policies and procedures or the by-laws, in recruitment manuals, in after dinner speeches, and in hallway conversations. The policy should explicitly include discussions of providing multiple helping resources for women as a matter of organizational policy.

This frequently announced commitment from the top is important for several reasons. Obviously all important organizational policies will be enunciated from the top in every significant organization, and equal opportunity must be seen to be important if it is to work.

Appropriate male-female relations at work must be legitimated. Traditionally socialized men and women may have very mixed feelings about whether it is really moral and proper for women to succeed in paid employment. Moreover whether or not an individual feels women should be equally successful as men, there may be discomfort or hesitancy about equal paths to success. A senior man (or woman) may cause adverse comment if he (or she) takes on a person of the opposite sex as a protégé. Senior people will feel free to become excellent mentors on a cross-sex basis only if their own bosses expect this to occur as part of excellent work performance.

Responsible, effective leadership in encouraging senior people to be mentors of course requires that a top administration encourage mentorship of all junior people. I do not recommend a separate special guidance program for women. Special programs of this kind are of questionable legality and morality and often lack long-term credibility and influence. What women do need is an explicit legitimation of their equal right to guidance and sponsors. They also frequently need the

---

2. Elsewhere I have written of two other institutional structures I consider indispensable to establishing an effective equal opportunity ecology: nonunion grievance procedures and a 1:1 recruitment system.

24

extra supports provided by women's networks and specific attention to women within general programs.

FOSTERING RESPONSIBLE NETWORKS OF WOMEN

As part of the organizational policy on equal opportunity and as an integral part of building mentorship frameworks, responsible women's networks should be encouraged. Grass roots networks of this kind have been repeatedly shown to be indispensable to sustained progress for blacks and women. Intraorganizational and interorganizational networks share information, provide mutual support, teach skills, and function as informal channels for inquiries and grievances. Such networks may provide the only reliable information on equal opportunity concerns that reaches top administrators. They will let top management know quickly which helping resources are most needed and where. Women's groups tend also to cool out socially irresponsible members, while providing leverage to those with responsible concerns and complaints. Finally, these groups are efficient at providing role models as well as sponsors for their members, even in organizations where there are only a very few senior women.

MAINTAINING CLOSE RELATIONS BETWEEN WOMEN'S NETWORKS AND TOP ADMINISTRATORS

Networks of women do grow, whether or not they are encouraged. Where they are fostered and respected and consulted, they are a powerful force for nonpolarized and steady progress. Covert, defensive groups, on the other hand, tend to polarize issues because they can see no alternatives. Then mentorship, coaching, and role models can become quite <u>negative</u> factors as polarization increases. Polarization often leads to backlash, and damage from backlash, of a kind many people would prefer to avoid. Moreover, covert networks cannot function efficiently to prevent trouble by an orderly presentation of concerns and grievances. Individuals who have serious complaints need clear channels for presenting their concerns if they are not to turn to the courts and other methods of taking things in their own hands.

Maintaining close communications between the top and the women's networks permits each group to learn from the other. Male managers learn what women want and need and what their special concerns are. Women learn

what is realistically available to them, about budget
constraints; they learn how to focus and balance their
own issues in a general perspective, and how the system
works.

TRAINING OF WOMEN TO FIND THEIR OWN SOURCES OF HELP

Feminists have long discussed the importance for
women of their taking responsibility and having some
control over their own careers. In practice this is
also the only effective way of finding adequate mentorship for women. The best framework for women to learn
what they need to know about productive and successful
careers requires that all junior women be specifically
taught and encouraged to seek their own guides and
sponsors. Junior women will be able to find adequate
mentorship much more easily if it is legitimated and
fostered by top administrators and women's networks.
But it is also critical that they themselves be receptive, that they seek out the guides, sponsors, and
coaches they need to reach their goals. Junior women
can be taught to do this by written guidelines, work-
shops, senior people, supervisors, and each other.
(See Appendix A: Go Find Yourself A Mentor, for an
example.)

BUILDING SPECIFIC MENTORSHIP PROGRAMS

Specific programs to encourage sponsorship,
guidance, and coaching are vital for employees everywhere, and for faculty and students as well, in educational institutions. Mentorship programs should be
designed:
1. for everyone, male and female, minority and
nonminority, good performers and poor performers,
faculty, staff, students, and employees, and there
should be specific safeguards to be sure such programs
work at least equally well for women and minorities;
2. around a performance evaluation program;
3. with a component to be sure someone is teaching women and minorities to seek and be receptive to
mentorship, so that mentors and protégés are seeking
each other simultaneously;

4. uniquely for the needs of each different
institution, each different pay classification, each
type of student.

A good mentorship program should be for everyone.
For example, in a university the concept of mentorship
needs to be developed for employees, especially support
staff, as well as for faculty and students. Mentorship
must be a part of the local ecology, an attitude toward
everyone, a part of a systematic framework of support
for career development and lifetime growth for everyone,
or it will not be effective for minorities and women, who
are usually located in inferior positions. Eroding occupational segregation requires that powerful levers for
change, like mentorship programs, extend across pay
classification lines.

Programs need to be for white males as well as for
minorities and women. Most people find general programs
more acceptable, more likely to be considered legal, and
more easily understood. General programs are also necessary to create a systematic framework for emphasis on
career development. Also, the most effective mentors
in any given environment are likely to be people who are
indigenous to that environment. White males are probably
the most influential mentors in a research university,
black females may be the best mentors in an inner city
day care center, and so on. Thus the enthusiastic support of white males for the mentorship program in a university will be very important for everyone. Equal
effectiveness for minorities and women can be fostered
by having programs designed and monitored by minority
and female staff as well as others, but the programs
need to be general.

Programs should be for poorer performers as well as
good ones. For example, it is vital to provide guidance
for junior faculty who are good enough to be promoted and
tenured, but it is even more important to provide excellent
mentorship for junior faculty who will not be kept. Every
such person should leave the college or university to a
good job, having been helped by mentors to plan realistically
and successfully for the future. Such support means that
those who leave will continue to speak well of the original
institution, which is important for recruiting. Peaceful
severance means lower costs for the original institution,
and, most important, going to something, rather than being

27

rejected, enhances the life of the individual who must
leave, instead of causing pain and damage.

A good mentorship program should begin with a discussion for every junior person with his or her supervisor,
e.g., faculty advisor, department head, twice a year. Corporations usually have some kind of regular performance
appraisal system; universities often do not provide even
this much feedback and support to junior people.

An adequate performance appraisal or mentorship discussion should include at least the following points:

1. Where has the junior person been doing well?
2. How could he or she do better?
3. Where does the supervisor or department head
think the job is going? (What will the needs of the
department be?)
4. What does the junior person want from the future?
What skills are being used? How would this person like to
grow on the job and in future jobs?

For faculty members, these discussions should include
frank appraisals of the possibilities for promotion and
tenure, sources of grant funds, identification of possible
mentors around the country or around the world, and so on.
For administrative and research and support staff, these
discussions should be specific and detailed as to strengths
and weaknesses, other possible sources of help, potential
career ladders.

Supervisory feedback should thus form the backbone of
mentorship programs in every institution. Few institutions
and especially few universities have made sure that career
development for junior people is a major and mandatory
component of performance evaluation discussions.

Institutions should identify people who can work with
junior members of the community, to teach them how to seek
adequate advice and mentorship. Women and minorities
particularly need to have someone who will legitimate and
foster their search for adequate guidance--a dean, an
assistant to the president, a vice president for personnel,
or any other senior person.

The purpose is to create an atmosphere in which the
institution requires senior people to give guidance and
encourages junior people to seek guidance. It is only
in such circumstances that cross-sex, cross-race diffi-
dence on both sides will be transcended, and that minorities and women will get adequate sponsorship.

Some institutions simply assign mentors on a first-year or permanent basis. Temporary assignments can be very helpful, but I believe long-term mentorships work best, at least in universities, if they develop naturally in a context where both parties are supposed to be looking for each other. I recommend that, instead of assigning mentors, an institution assign a few people to teach the acquisition of mentorship to juniors while monitoring performance evaluation by seniors.

Good mentorship programs should be built around the specific needs and customs of each organization to specifically accommodate different kinds of employees and students. For example, guidance and support to people in postdoctoral positions must occur within the customs of each different discipline and be tailored to a specific university's expectations of principal investigators. Mentorship for administrators in a small college may require someone with considerable knowledge of the regional labor market. A person who is teaching junior faculty to develop their own mentors must be finely tuned to different practices in each discipline. Custom tailoring in this way is not particularly difficult; in fact it is easier than trying to graft a mentorship program from one institution onto another. Usually there are very successful people in each field who are glad to be able to advise on how programs should develop in their own laboratory or department or agency.

Institutions that show leadership in this new area have everything to gain. Doubling the available pool of skills and abilities is vital to the success of most organizations. In addition most institutions employ and serve women. They can do so more profitably and efficiently by understanding better their female employees and clients. If they do so ahead of their competitors they can gain an enviable reputation that lasts for generations and helps to continue attracting the ablest faculty and employees, students and clients. As we plan for coming years, the practice of true equal opportunity is patently less costly, in terms of litigation, emotional damage, and other problems. Since mentorship frameworks appear to be as important for women as they always have been for men, institutions stand only to gain by building such frameworks in an orderly, responsible fashion.

DISCUSSION

Support for Junior People. One participant noted that MIT differs from many other institutions of higher education in its philosophy of hiring. Because there is no fixed number of tenured positions at MIT as there is elsewhere, each person appointed to an assistant professorship could potentially achieve tenure. The question is how can that person's colleagues help him or her make the grade. At other institutions, in contrast, the six-year trial period is often just that, a test to see whether or not the person can make it. This makes an extraordinary difference in the kinds of help extended to a junior person.

Bernice Sandler concurred. "If a person is hired with the expectation that he or she will make it, then the mentor relationship is much more likely to develop between that person and the senior colleagues," she said. Sandler observed that mentors are not annointed or, as a rule, appointed. The protégé has to take the responsibility for finding a mentor and asking for help. Also, she noted, sometimes no mentor can be found. Either the people are too busy, or you can't find them, or there is some other obstacle. There are alternative ways of getting information and help, she said. In the women's movement, women advise one another as equals, sharing technical information on proposal writing, for instance. There are other support groups and sources of information, as well. She suggested that perhaps the first step is to define the kinds of things one needs to know. One can approach a mentor to help answer that question, to say, "I'm going to be here for the next couple of years. What are the kinds of things I ought to know and learn?" You could list some and ask if you missed any, Sandler said.

Sex Roles and Mentors. A participant noted that older males are sometimes leery of taking on a young woman as a protégé for fear their relationship will be misunderstood. Fessenden-Raden and Sandler concurred that this can be a problem. Fessenden-Raden pointed to the emphasis in Rowe's paper on legitimizing the relationship to avoid that kind of criticism. Every person at the conference, Fessenden-Raden guessed, had had the experience of having lunch with a member of the opposite sex and having a colleague come along and make some kind of wise remark. We have, also, the dramatic case of Mary Cunningham whose meteoric rise to a vice presidency caused such upheaval at the Bendix Corporation. This underlines the importance of the top managers saying, "We expect this kind of interaction." Fessenden-Raden added that it seems important for a protégé to get to know his or her mentor's family. (Several participants noted here that Mary Cunningham had in fact done that and it had not helped her any.)

Sandler also commented on the Cunningham case, noting that (1) she was not fired because she had a mentor. She resigned because she moved up through the ranks very very quickly and that had engendered hostility and political struggles among those she had overtaken and passed. (2) The second interesting aspect of Mary Cunningham's resignation was the amount of controversy it provoked. The Washington Post and the Washington Star both had articles by Gail Sheehey; there were letters to the editor; editorials were published Interesting questions (perhaps not interesting to Cunningham but to others) were raised, such as "If she had been ugly, would this have happened? What happens to a woman who becomes the first woman promoted to that level?" Both women and men have been talking about these issues and that's good. Cunningham herself is sturdy and she has had, Sandler noted, many, many job offers.

Other Problems with Mentors. What do you do, one participant asked, if your mentor is a dud? Sandler responded that your mentor does not have to be a star. Mary Rowe mentioned "multiple resources" in her paper; one can also think of "multiple mentors," Sandler said. If a person can give you advice and help on some subject that you care about, you should make that person your mentor even if nobody else thinks his or her expertise is worth anything. To be sure, that person can't give you counsel on how to move up in the system since he or she hasn't gone that route. But that person may have some valuable insights because he or she has seen the system from a perspective different from those of people who are desperately trying to make it in the system. It isn't always good to choose a mentor because he or she has the appearance of success. The issue is, What can that person tell you that will help you? And how can you repay that? Not by giving it back to your mentor, but by being a mentor to someone else.

Sexual Harassment. A graduate student brought up the
problem of establishing a relationship in an all-male
department trusting enough to discuss problems such as
incidents of sexual harassment. Both Fessenden-Raden
and Sandler acknowledged this as a real problem.
Fessenden-Raden suggested looking outside one's own
department for a woman faculty member—even if she is
not tenured—for counsel or, alternatively, turning to
a male faculty member and getting to know his family.
Sandler advised defusing the sexual aspects of a relationship by not going to a mentor by oneself. Two or
three or more women could go to a male faculty member
and ask him out for a beer. Once out, you can convey
to him that you need his help professionally and that
you are not interested in him as a sexual object. A
second possibility is to choose a faculty man who is
both (1) respected in the department so people will
listen to him and (2) sufficiently sensitive to be
educable in these matters. Two or three of you go to
him and tell him the problem. You might begin by saying that you know the department cares about women
because you are there, but that the women need and want
the kind of help mentors give. Ask his advice on how
to approach the department on this issue.

The student responded that she felt that, if one
has a problem with sexual harassment, one would feel
most comfortable in going to a woman for counsel as to
how to handle it. Sandler concurred, noting that one
probably shouldn't seek out a male mentor to resolve
this problem. If one has a mentor already, he could
give comfort and advice, however. Her project, she
noted, has written a paper on this subject.[3]

Multiple Mentors. A tenured woman noted that she had
never had a problem finding mentors in part because she
defined the issue the way Rowe's paper advises: multiple
sources. She approached her department (in a college of
home economics that had, at that time, all male full
professors except for one female who had come through the
extension division) in the belief that individuals would
be willing to help her. They were. She had some mentors

---

3. This paper and others on related subjects are available
from the Project on the Status and Education of Women,
Association of American Colleges, 1818 R Street NW, Washington, D.C. 20009.

who provided technical assistance with papers and research, she said, and others to whom she turned for help when in emotional trouble or when needing advice on strategy and tactics. A tenured male faculty member commented that the mentoring relationship had never been studied from the perspective of the mentor. Who are these mentors? he wondered. This question is addressed by the Garrison and Davis master's thesis for the MIT Sloan School. The faculty member also cited a book by Levinson, The Seasons of a Man's Life, that defines mentorship as a stage in one's development.[4] An interesting question might be the "rise and fall of a mentor," he noted. How do mentors learn to be able to let their protégés go?

A particular problem for which mentorship might not be a viable solution is the way in which women's studies research is defined, one student noted. Sandler concurred. When she had wanted to undertake studies of women, she was told that that was not "real research," she said. An individual mentor cannot perhaps help one to solve that systemwide problem, she said.

Mentorship should provide information about jobs available, one participant noted; a second said another key component is the sharing of information about financial resources available. Fessenden-Raden noted that an individual can have mentors in different departments, in different universities, even in different countries. Sandler added that some mentor relationships can be short-term and others longer. One could meet a mentor just once or perhaps only several times--or one could turn to him or her for the rest of one's life. Mentorship is, a participant concluded, teaching in the very highest sense. A conference like the present one provides an opportunity to not only find a mentor but to be one.

---

4. Daniel J. Levinson et al., The Seasons of a Man's Life (New York: Alfred A. Knopf, 1978).

3.
Grievances and Their Redress in the Eighties

Helen C. Davies and Robert E. Davies

HISTORY

At the turn of the century women represented 8
percent of the full professors at the University of
Chicago whereas in 1968-69 only 2 percent of the full
professors were women.[1] The records of the mathematics
department of the University of California at Berkeley
show that in 1928 women held 20 percent of the tenured
or tenure-accruing positions. In 1938 the figure was
down to 11 percent; in 1948 it was 7 percent; in 1958
it was 3 percent; and in 1969 it was zero.[2] During
the period from 1920 to 1929, 10 percent of the doctorates in mathematics awarded by the department were
received by women, and between 1960 and 1968 the figure
was 6 percent. Of the approximately four thousand

This contribution reviews the highlights of and updates
a paper given in 1978 at a conference sponsored by the
New York Academy of Sciences and the Association for
Women in Science Education Foundation. H. C. Davies
and R. E. Davies, "Redress of Grievances," in Expanding
the Role of Women in the Sciences, A. M. Briscoe and S. M.
Pfafflin, eds., Annals of the New York Academy of Sciences
323 (1979):197-209.

1. P. A. Graham, "Women in Academe," Science 169 (1970):
1284-90.

2. Science and Government Report 1 (Daniel S. Greenberg,
June 1, 1971), 1.

full-time staff in chemistry departments in this
country offering doctoral studies, the number of
women in 1974-75 was 88 or 2.2 percent.[3] In the
latest survey the American Chemical Society reported
that during the 1978-79 academic year 129 women were
assistant professors or above on these faculties,
representing 3.0 percent of the total.[4] By contrast,
11 percent of Ph.D. graduating classes over the past
ten years were women (180 per year). Of the total
of 188 doctorate-granting chemistry departments in
1978-79, 96 had no women. In 1978 Nixon, a past
president of the American Chemical Society, reported
that there were only 19 full-time women chemistry
professors in the whole country and only one in the
Ivy League schools, our colleague Madeleine Joullié
of the University of Pennsylvania.[5]

A major problem has been the long history of
actions that have been perceived differently by most
males and most females or have been embedded in generally accepted societal values. Many engineers,
chemists, veterinarians, and mathematicians were convinced beyond rational argument that theirs was a male
profession and only the most unusual women could enter
and be successful. The existence of "old boys' networks," the ready assumptions that a search committee
should find the best man for a position and that women
were incompetent, not serious, and should be at home all
helped perpetuate the present discriminatory situation.
This view is what Naomi McAfee termed "an old husband's
tale."[6]

3. A. C. Nixon, "Changing Attitudes towards Women in the
Profession of Chemistry," in Expanding the Role of Women
in the Sciences, A. M. Briscoe and S. M. Pfafflin, eds.,
Annals of the New York Academy of Sciences 323:146-72.

4. Chemical and Engineering News, June 2, 1980, p. 28.

5. Nixon, "Changing Attitudes in Chemistry."

6. Stated during McAfee's presentation to the 1978 conference Expanding the Role of Women in the Sciences, but
not published in her paper.

The beginning of the turnabout for women came with the passage of the federal law protecting them against sex discrimination in 1964 when Howard W. Smith, chairman of the Rules Committee of the U.S. House of Representatives added the word sex to Title VII of the Civil Rights Act. Although widely accepted as a joke and as a device to divide the liberals and prevent the passage of the bill, Title VII became law.[7] The federal laws and regulations concerning sex discrimination in educational institutions are Executive Order 11246 as amended by Executive Order 11375, Title VII of the Civil Rights Act, the Equal Pay Act of 1963, Title IX of the Education Amendments of 1972 (Higher Education Act), and Titles VII and VIII of the Public Health Service Act.[8] Under Executive Order 11246 as amended by Executive Order 11375, affirmative action plans including "numerical goals and timetables are required of all contractors with contracts of more than $50,000 or 50 or more employees."

Until the passage of this legislation it was virtually impossible to obtain redress of grievances brought on the grounds of sex discrimination since nobody had or has the right to an appointment, promotion, or tenure. Nowadays, at least when appointments and promotions are made, the law requires that they should not be discriminatory with regard to sex, race, creed, age, handicap, and so forth. This also applies to salary levels.

---

7. C. Bird, Born Female (New York: Pocket Books, 1971).

8. A chart of these laws has been prepared and updated (June 1977) by the Association of American Colleges' Project on the Status and Education of Women. Federal Laws and Regulations concerning Sex Discrimination in Educational Institutions (Washington, D.C.: Department of Health, Education and Welfare, Office for Civil Rights, 1977). Also a very fine discussion of the laws may be found in B. Sandler, "A Little Help from Our Government: WEAL and Contract Compliance," in A. S. Rossi and A. Calderwood, eds., Academic Women on the Move (New York: Russell Sage Foundation, 1973), pp. 439-504.

SUBSTANTIATION OF SEX DISCRIMINATION

In order to substantiate a claim of sex discrimination a first step is to look for evidence that women are discriminated against at the hiring level in the institution concerned. There is empirical verification of sex discrimination in hiring practices in the scientific academic community. In the field of psychology, for instance, Fidell has shown that academic departments of psychology in 1970 discriminated on the basis of sex.[9] In this study either of two forms, A or B, was sent to the chairman of each of 228 colleges and universities. Each form described the professional history of hypothetical psychologists, and the chairmen were asked to judge the candidates' chances of getting a position. Forms A and B differed in that some of the candidates who were women in one form were described as men in the other and vice versa. The chairmen's responses were such that the modal level of potential offers of position for the women was assistant professor, while for the men it was associate professor. Only the men would have been offered full professorships.

In another study made in 1968, Simpson submitted pairs of resumés to administrators with the descriptive material held constant and the names and photographs of women and men alternated on the two forms. He reported that deans, chairmen, and faculty in selected academic fields at six institutions in Pennsylvania rated the men higher than the women.[10]

In 1971 Lewin and Duchan did a similar study of chairmen of graduate departments of a physical science discipline in institutions of higher education. The chairmen preferred an average male over an average female, but did recognize a clearly superior woman candidate. A significant number of unsolicited comments were returned with the questionnaires accompanying the resumés of the women. The chairmen expressed concern about the fate of the applicant's husband and children. They were also concerned with her compatibility

---

9. L. S. Fidell, "Empirical Verification of Sex Discrimination in Hiring Practices in Psychology," American Psychology 25 (1970):1094-98.

10. L. Simpson, "A Study of Employing Agents' Attitudes toward Academic Women in Higher Education" (Ph.D. dissertation, Pennsylvania State University, 1968).

with their department members, leading the authors to state that women faculty in the physical sciences may be evaluated on the basis of different criteria than are men when they compete for academic positions.[11]

Marcus held in 1976 that despite the recent widespread use of advertisements for academic positions the network approach is still the most important recruitment means in academe. Since the network among senior faculty is predominantly white male, the persistence of this approach as a major technique for identifying promising candidates inevitably leads to a disproportionate hiring of protégés who are also white and male.[12]

To substantiate further the claim of sex discrimination, evidence should be obtained showing that the number of women hired and promoted at particular levels in a given department is not proportional to the number of women with advanced degrees and appropriate experience in that field. The basic source of our faculty is the pool of scholars who have earned doctorates in the United States. There is ample statistical information on this pool.[13] In an example of the use of availability figures,

---

11. A. Y. Lewin and L. Duchan, "Women in Academia," Science 173 (1971):892-95.

12. L. R. Marcus, "Has Advertising Produced Results in Faculty Hiring?" Educational Record 57, 4 (1976).

13. See H. S. Astin, "Career Profiles of Women Doctorates," in A. S. Rossi and A. Calderwood, eds., Academic Women on the Move (New York: Russell Sage Foundation, 1973), pp. 139-79; Minorities and Women in the Health Fields, DHEW Publication (HRA) 76-22 (Washington, D.C.: U.S. Department of Health, Education and Welfare, Public Health Service, 1975); E. Burnett, Doctors Degrees Conferred by All U.S. Institutions: By State, Academic Field, Sex, and Institution 1964-65 through 1973-74 (Washington, D.C.: U.S. Department of Health, Education and Welfare, Office of Education, 1975); Manual for Determining the Labor Market Availability of Women and Minorities (Washington, D.C.: U.S. Department of Health, Education and Welfare, Office of the Secretary, Office for Civil Rights, 1974); Manpower Resources for Scientific Activities at Universities and Colleges (Washington, D.C.: National Science Foundation), 1975); B. M.

data produced in a study of the coeducational University
of Pennsylvania by a committee on the status of women
in 1971 showed that in the college there were 164 male
full professors and no women full professors.[14] Of
eighty-eight departments, forty-eight had not one woman.
Using the information on the number of doctorates earned
in the respective fields of study for the appropriate
years as an estimate of the proportion of qualified
women in each discipline, a comparison was made with the
proportion of faculty women found in departments at the
university. Out of thirty-three departments for which
this comparison could be made, twenty-six had less than
the expected figure. Even ignoring the fact that most
of these departments had no women at all, the probability
of this distribution occurring by chance is 6.6 x 10^{-7}.

Of course it is helpful in substantiating a claim
of sex discrimination if the woman is Superwoman, has
an outstanding publication list in first-rate refereed
journals either as first or sole author, has been ex-
tensively cited, and is widely recognized. The problem
is greater for the merely excellent and good women
compared with the equivalent men. The present profes-
soriat, chairpersons and external referees, promotions
committees, deans, and provosts' staffs are overwhelmingly male. Although they nowadays usually deny any sex
bias, the results of their actions do not satisfy most
women in academe.

CRITERIA

In 1973 a committee of the Women's Faculty Club at
the University of Pennsylvania examined virtually all

Vetter, Supply and Demand for Scientists and Engineers--A
Review of Selected Studies (Washington, D.C.: Scientific
Manpower Commission, 1977); Doctoral Scientists and
Engineers in the United States 1975 Profile (Washington,
D.C.: National Research Council, National Academy of
Science, 1975).

14. "Report of the Committee on the Status of Women,
Women Faculty in the University of Pennsylvania: Parts
1, 2, 3," Almanac, University of Pennsylvania, April 13,
20, 27, 1971.

the possible ways of determining excellence or quality
in academe and decided that nearly all of them had a
strong built-in sex bias. Even now most of them still
have a sex bias. A list of these criteria follows.

Personal and Professional History
1. Present rank and title. At what
college or university. Rate at which
the person progressed through the ranks.

2. Where the doctorate or other professional degree was obtained.

3. Membership in important departmental,
school, and university committees.
Holding an office on these committees.

4. Administrative responsibilities in
the university.

5. Serving as a consultant, specialist,
advisor, trustee to universities, hos-
pitals, federal, state and city agencies,
industry, foundations, etc.

6. The integrated assessment of colleagues
concerning one's standing in the field.

7. Invitations to accept posts at other
universities or equivalent outstanding
institutions.

8. The contents of letters of evaluation written especially at the time
of appointment or promotion.

9. Appearance of one's name in _Ameri-
can Men and Women of Science_, _Directory
of American Scholars_, _World Who's Who in
Science_, _Who's Who_, etc.

10. Membership in prestigious state
and national professional societies and
academies; holding an office in these
societies.

Teaching
11. Evidence of good teaching based
on evaluation of present students,
past students, faculty.

40

12. The receiving of local and national awards and prizes for teaching.

13. Being assigned responsibility for advanced teaching, more specialized clinical duties, etc.

Scholarship and Research

14. The number and quality of papers, monographs, chapters in books, books, etc., published.

15. Papers published in good refereed journals, especially those with high rejection rates. (This should include citation frequency and impact factors, if possible, of the journals).

16. Number and type of citations of published papers.

17. Citation rate of each when compared with other people of comparable academic rank, in a similar discipline.

18. Number and quality of papers representing independent work--not with more prestigious authors.

19. Citation rate for such papers.

20. Citations in Annual Reviews of..., Advances in..., Progress in..., etc., and textbooks.

21. Number of papers presented at professional meetings by one's own decision.

22. Number of patents issued.

23. Having grants from National Institutes of Health, National Science Foundation, National Endowment for the Humanities, American Council of Learned Societies, etc. The amounts and frequency of these grants.

24. Invitations to give lectures at: other universities, national meetings, international meetings of societies, congresses, symposia, etc.

25. Invitations to write reviews of books or topics in important journals.

26. Being asked to be chair, discussant, organizer, keynote speaker at professional meetings.

27. Receiving honorary degrees, awards, prizes, medals, etc., from state, national, and international bodies.

28. Having methodological, chemical, surgical, etc., procedures, formulae and operations, etc., named after one.

29. Performances of one's plays, operas, and exhibitions of works.

30. Request rate for reprints from many states, countries, continents and different departments in and peripheral to the appropriate academic areas.

31. Reviews of one's books.

32. Invitations to act as referee for papers in important journals.

33. Invitation to be editor or member of the editorial board of appropriate journals.

34. Serving on study sections at the National Institutes of Health, etc., for reviewing grant applications.

35. Number of students who take research degrees with the person concerned.

36. The history of these students after graduation. How many have become professors, etc.

Other
37. Involvement in community activity, business, and other nonacademic experience.

Citation analysis is becoming more widely used to assess scientific work, and the recent availability of the Social Science Citation Index and the Arts and Humanities Citation Index in addition to the Science Citation Index will make this technique more widely available.[15] With many appropriate precautions the number of citations a paper receives in leading scientific journals can be taken as a measure of the use and importance of the work. With these precautions and an allowance for joint authorship, the citations to a paper represent an evaluation of the work by the totality of publishing scientists and thus form an objective measure of what has been variously described as the "effectiveness," "impact," "importance," "eminence," "influence," "quality," "significance," or "utilization" of the work. Much of the evidence for these claims is gathered in a paper entitled "Life-time Citation Rates to Compare Scientists' Work" by Geller, de Cani, and Davies.[16] These papers give a method by which the citation history of most new and old papers can be compared quantitatively and thus the scientific work of most young and older professors may be fairly compared. As J. A. Virgo wrote, "Citations actually reflect a consensus of a large group of readers as compared to the evaluation of a single individual." She also noted, "Those articles judged important by subject experts tended to be those cited frequently in the subsequent literature while those judged to be less important were those papers which had rarely been cited subsequently or had never been cited at all."[17] Meadows claimed, "The best

---

15. Science Citation Index, Social Sciences Citation Index, Arts and Humanities Citation Index (Philadelphia: Institute for Scientific Information, Inc.).

16. N. L. Geller, J. S. de Cani, and R. E. Davies, "Life-time-Citation Rates to Compare Scientists' Work: Past Citations to Most Scientific Papers Can Be Used to Predict Their Future Numbers of Citations," Social Science Research 7 (1978):345-65. See also N. L. Geller, J. S. de Cani, and R. E. Davies, "Lifetime-Citation Rates: A Mathematical Model to Compare Scientists' Work," Journal of the American Society for Information Science 31, 5 (1981):1-15.

17. J. A. Virgo (thesis, University of Chicago, 1974).

guide (of quality) seems to be the number of times a scientist's papers are cited."[18]

It is interesting that many published papers are never ever cited. The citation frequency distribution data from the 1978 Science Citation Index shows that of more than 3,800,000 cited items, 70 percent were cited only once.[19] Only 23 percent were cited 2 to 4 times. Those with 5 to 9 citations were in the 94.8^{th} percentile; 10 to 16, the 98.7^{th} percentile; 17 to 25, the 99.62^{nd} percentile; 26 to 50, the 99.81^{st} percentile; 51 to 100, the 99.96^{th} percentile. The 353 items cited more than 101 times were in the 99.99^{th} percentile.

These figures do not vary much from year to year. Figures like them allow one to compare the notice taken of any given paper with that of all the millions of cited papers in that year. Of course a more precise estimate would compare the citation performance of papers within a given field; this information is available for the most-cited papers in many fields and for the average paper in many journals, i.e., the "impact factor," the average citation rate per published item in that journal.[20]

WOMEN'S NETWORKS

Filing an internal grievance or going to federal court is a very serious matter. It is usually extremely wearing, oppressive, and expensive in terms of money, peace of mind, and friendships. Every effort should be made to resolve the problems informally, with a little bit or a lot of help from your friends and colleagues.

---

18. A. J. Meadows, Communication in Science (London: Butterworths, 1974). See also E. Garfield, Citation Indexing--Its Theory and Application in Science, Technology and Humanities (New York: John Wiley & Sons, 1979).

19. E. Garfield, "ABCs of Cluster Mapping: Part 1, Most Active Fields in the Life Sciences in 1978," Current Contents 40 (October 6, 1980), 5-12.

20. E. Garfield, Essays of an Information Scientist, 2 vols. (Philadelphia: Institute for Scientific Information Press, 1977).

Grievances and Their Redress

At some academic institutions women have established
their own networks. One such has been eloquently described by Karen Childers, Phyllis Rackin, Cynthia Secor,
and Carol Tracy in their article "A Network of One's Own,"
which relates the history of WEOUP (Women for Equal Opportunity at the University of Pennsylvania).[21] The goal of
the women is equality in campus life, and their few ground
rules are on race (that nothing asked for women be at the
expense of what is needed for minorities on the campus),
on violence (counterproductive), and on patience with women
not yet with them (Don't scratch a woman to find a sister;
the system will scratch her shortly. Be there to help).

WEOUP formally organized, raised funds, wrote bylaws,
hired an attorney, made contact with EEOC, filed a class
action suit (still pending) with both EEOC and the Common-
wealth Human Relations Commission. WEOUP negotiated a
position for itself as a review committee for administration proposals and policies on women; helped set up a
women's studies planning group, supported several women's
cases (several successful, several pending); coordinated
a national conference on women's studies; staged a successful four-day sit-in after five women were raped in three
days and the security director implied publicly that rape
is a woman's own fault; negotiated, as a result of the sit-
in, a women's center as headquarters for all women's activities, with two staff members and operating funds paid by
the university; worked on day care (with the result that
there is now a day care center); lobbied high-level administrators to resolve specific women's grievances; and much
more. Beyond these types of projects the group gives
specific help (from work flow analysis to proofreading
grant applications) and psychological encouragement ("So
you don't think you're great? To whom are you comparing
yourself, Einstein or the last product of the 'old boy' network your department hired?").

The most satisfactory way to redress a grievance may
well be to do it privately and internally, but this rarely
works. The presence of powerful friends, people who care
about justice and are not afraid to speak up and act, and
a local and national network of women are often crucial.

21. K. Childers, P. Rackin, C. Secor, and C. Tracy, A Network of One's Own (New York: Modern Language Association
of America, in press).

GRIEVANCES

If all the above criteria and a proper citation
analysis fail to win the support due a woman faculty
member, then attempts may reasonably be made to redress
the grievance.

After exhausting the normal channels of appeal to
the chair of the department and the dean of the school,
the office of the ombudsman, if it exists, may be helpful.
The University of Pennsylvania has had such an office
since 1971, and every year since then several hundred
members of the university community—students, staff,
administrative and faculty members—have sought help
from the ombudsman. Annual reports from this office
make interesting reading.[22] This onerous and very
important position has been filled by four white male
professors in succession. About 10 percent of the
complaints were from faculty members, and of these a
dozen cases that reached the Faculty Grievance Commission
could not be resolved by informal negotiations.

One of us, Robert Davies, was a member of all the
various committees and subcommittees that wrote and re-
wrote the faculty grievance procedure of the University

----

22. J. Conarroe, "Dissonance and Discourse: Notes from
a Windy Room," First Annual Report of the Office of the
Ombudsman, 1971-72, Almanac, University of Pennslyvania,
October 3, 1972; J. Conarroe, "I'm Okay, You're Okay:
The Second Annual Report of the Ombudsman, 1972-73,"
Almanac, September 4, 1973; J. O. Freedman, "An Ombuds-
man's Angle of Vision," Third Annual Report of the Office
of the Ombudsman, 1973-74, Almanac, September 17, 1974;
J. O. Freedman, "The Ombudsman as Go-Between," Fourth
Annual Report of the Office of the Ombudsman, 1974-75,
Almanac, September 9, 1975; J. O. Freedman, "What Purpose
Does an Ombudsman Serve?," Fifth Annual Report of the
Ombudsman, Almanac, May 11, 1976; J. Abel, "An Ombudsman's
Potpourri," Report of the Office of the Ombudsman 1975-78,
Almanac, January 23, 1979, University of Pennslyvania; and
J. C. Keene, "Reflections on Conflict Resolution and Norm
Enforcement at the University of Pennslyvania," Report of
the Office of the Ombudsman, 1978-80, Almanac, November
18, 1980.

of Pennsylvania and helped steer it through the Faculty
Senate and University Council. It became operative in
May 1974, and Robert Davies served as chairman of the
Faculty Grievance Commission for the first two years and
as a member until the procedure was superseded.

At the New York conference mentioned earlier we gave
details of the working of the faculty grievance procedure
at the University of Pennsylvania. This procedure has
since been changed because we found by bitter experience
in a case involving a woman's grievance that we had no
effective internal mechanism for dealing with the situation
when the administration refused to operate the procedures
properly and fairly.[23] The dispute went to court and was
settled satisfactorily without a hearing. The Faculty
Grievance Commission then refused to operate the old procedure, and after much committee work, the Faculty Senate
eventually agreed to a new one in November 1978 (see
Appendix B).[24]

Of course not all complaints go to the grievance commission. The office of the ombudsman at Penn receives
by far the largest number, and it has dealt with, for
example, the problems of sexual harassment. This is an
"increasingly visible" problem[25] which inspite of the
remarkably insensitive and inaccurate claims of George H.
Douglas is not "a tempest in a teapot", nor is it true
that "women have never needed, and do not now need, the

---

23. R. E. Davies, "The Faculty Grievance Commission--The
First Year," Almanac, University of Pennslyvania, May 20,
1975; R. E. Davies, "The Faculty Grievance Commission--The
Second Year," Almanac, November 2, 1976; S. Green, "Report
of the Faculty Grievance Commission, July 1976--March 1978,"
Almanac, April 11, 1978; D. Hurvich, P. Mechanick, C. Oliver,
and P. Taubman, "Report of the Senate Advisory Committee
Board of Review for the Grievance Commission," Almanac, April
11, 1978; R. E. Davies, "Modifications in the Grievance Mechanism," Almanac, April 11, 1978.

24. "Faculty Grievance Procedure" (Philadelphia: University
of Pennsylvania, 1974, 1978). See Appendix B.

25. L. Middleton, "Harassment by Professors: An Increasingly
Visible Problem," Chronicle of Higher Education 21, 4 (September 15, 1980):1,4.

help of committees, tribunals, and snooper boards."[26]
Our certain knowledge is that all too many powerless
women, especially students and junior faculty members,
need all the help they can get in this area. Even
Douglas stated in parentheses that "Well, of course
I agree, that such 'blackmailers' as these are should
be hauled before some magistrate." Hauling someone
before a magistrate may well be futile and self-destruct-
ive, given the conditions under which sexual harassment
occurs.

Other formal procedures available to the faculty at
the University of Pennsylvania include the very important
senate and school committees on academic freedom and
responsibility; the University Court, which has original
jurisdiction over cases involving infractions of the
Guidelines on Open Expression; and the office of equal
opportunity. There are also formal mechanisms for "remov-
al by reason of financial exigency," "procedures for suspension or termination for just cause," and reviews of
claims for long-term disability.

As an ex-ombudsman said recently, the attacks on academic freedom come much more from some chairpersons of
departments rather than from the trustees, and we have
routine, if not as yet very efficient or effective methods
of regular reviews of all administrators and chairpersons.
Although the University of Pennsylvania is a long way from
being perfect, it is better for handling grievances than
most other places we know.

Grievance procedures at other universities vary enor-
mously. Most allow grievances to be initiated based on
claims of discrimination on account of race, sex, creed,
or national origin; some include political conviction,
handicap, age, or even membership in, e.g., the American
Association of University Professors (AAUP). The AAUP
itself has one of the most inclusive lists. The association's council approved the following in October 1976:
"The Association is committed to use its procedures and to
take measures including censure against colleges and universities practicing illegal or unconstitutional discrimination on a basis not demonstrably related to the job

---

26. G. H. Douglas to the editor, Chronicle of Higher
Education 21, 9 (October 20, 1980), p. 24.

function involved, including but not limited to age,
sex, physical handicap, race, religion, national origin,
marital status or sexual or affectional preference."[27]
The phrase "sexual or affectional preference," was only
recently included in the University of Pennsylvania procedure.

The mechanisms for investigation vary widely, are
frequently vague, and usually heavily weighted towards
the administration. In some cases the president, provost,
or dean determines the composition of the investigating
committee, fixes the rules of procedure, and can accept
or reject the conclusions. In others the committee is
selected from past members of a faculty council by a
committee on academic freedom, or by the faculty of the
university or school. Many of these people or bodies are
overwhelmingly white males, some of whom may well not be
sensitive to the special problems of women and minority
groups.

In a few cases, the grievant may have a right of
selection of at least one member of the investigating
committee, although the selection may be from, say,
present and past members of the faculty council and only
rarely from the whole university faculty. Most places
have no provision for peremptory challenge of the members
or even for challenge for cause.

The rules of procedure are often vague and inadequate
and rarely allow the grievant to be present during the investigation, hear evidence, call witnesses, cross-examine
opposing witnesses, or either directly, or indirectly,
through an advisor or colleague, have access to the relevant documents and files. In some cases grievants remain
alone, in others they may have a university colleague or
counsel present who may speak for them. In some the right
to counsel applies to witnesses too and occasionally to the
provost or dean or whoever is defending the case for the
administration.

In nearly all cases the report goes to the dean, provost, or president, who then decides what to do. Few institutions allow further appeals to the president, the
trustees or the committee on academic freedom in the event
that the university official rejects the decisions or
recommendations of the investigating committee.

---

27. "On Discrimination," Policy Documents and Reports (Washington, D.C.: American Association of University Professors,
1977), p. 22.

It is sadly clear that what passes for due process at many academic institutions is extremely unsatisfactory, unfair, and heavily weighted in favor of the status quo and the administration. Where the provost or the dean is also the affirmative action officer, the chance of significant conflicts of interest may well be high.

In some universities the faculty has designated the American Association of University Professors, the National Educational Association, or some other body as the exclusive collective bargaining agent. The agreements usually include many internal processes, but may also lead to binding arbitration. This, like a court decision, can compel the administration to act. It remains to be seen, however, whether arbitrators, who, like federal judges, are predominantly older white males, will act in cases involving claims of discrimination with respect to sex in ways perceived to be fair by members of the various organizations of professional women.

COURTROOM DEFENSES OF DISCRIMINATORY PRACTICES

So far the procedures have not generally been perceived by women as resulting in equitable treatment. Women who protest, file grievances, or go to court are almost uniformly disappointed, bitter and in financial and personal distress. They become known as "trouble makers," are blacklisted, and frequently have the greatest difficulty or even find it impossible to remain active in their chosen profession.[28]

Despite help from the Association for Women in Science (AWIS), the National Organization for Women (NOW) and its legal defense fund, Women's Equity Action League (WEAL), various state human relations commissions, the Equal Employment Opportunity Commission (EEOC), and the U.S. Department of Health, Education and Welfare (HEW), trials in federal courts can easily take years to resolve, cost many hundreds of hours of administraotrs' and faculty members' time, and cost hundreds of thousands of dollars. They can also result in much unfavorable publicity to all concerned. Much of the remuneration, if any, seems to go to the attorneys.

---

28. A. Theodore, "Academic Women in Protest," in progress.

Although some institutions have gone through this whole process and have usually won the legal battle, several have chosen to settle out of court by negotiation. These include most of the cases that have come to a reasonably satisfactory conclusion. In our view, it is clearly necessary to improve procedures and morality and thus the chance of justice being done.

From a direct knowledge of many grievance cases in many parts of the United States, some internal to the educational institutions and some that have reached the courts, we are distressed at the behavior of some professors, chairpersons, deans, provosts, presidents, and trustees in the last few years. This behavior has included failure to operate and abide by the grievance procedures, attacks on the integrity of members of hearing committees, broken promises, lies (even under oath), and deception. More specifically, the incidents have involved severe harassment, deliberate solicitation of favorable letters for men and unfavorable ones for women, alteration of letters of recommendation--positively for men and negatively for women--the suppression of unfavorable letters and student comments concerning men, the suppression of favorable letters and student comments concerning women, the use of tailor-made advertisements for positions so that only a specific male candidate fits the position description completely, the falsification of curriculum vitaes, the suppression of the results of departmental and promotion committee votes, the publication by men of professional women's research work without acknowledgment or joint authorship, and the denigration of a woman's research and claim that it did not fit into the mission of the department or school--even though that identical line of research was accepted for the initial appointment and was being pursued in many other equivalent institutions.

If the matter gets to court the problems multiply, and there are publications advising administrators on how to win cases and make it as difficult as possible for the plaintiff. For example, Stitt and Limitone published a paper discussing the strategies and tactics that they have found useful in defending institutions against litigation over claims of sex discrimination. It is worth examining the techniques that at least some institutions find acceptable. Stitt and Limitone say that often the person against whom the complaint is

being made (the respondent) and the concerned government
official may be known to each other from religious, community, or other activities. As a result of this acquaint-
ance the government official may ask for an off-the-record
meeting without lawyers about the complaint. The authors
state, "Indeed, we have yet to be embarrassed by such informal approaches which often result in resolving immedi-
ately unjustified complaints."[29]

Concerning the demand for university records, the
authors say that these demands are always subject to discussion and negotiation. With regard to conciliation
efforts, they note that conciliation is a"...convenient
and appropriate means of gaining time...." Since, they
say, HEW compliance review teams do not tend to become
involved during the conciliation stage, more time can be
gained.

They recommend pleading as a defense by a university
that the complainant has failed to exhaust a union contract or an intrauniversity grievance procedure. It is
clear that one of their important defenses is to demonstrate that universities are unique institutions and
that complaints against them should be handled differently from the way complaints are handled against business corporations. They discuss the way to prevent the
complainant from using a hearing for discovery of necessary data that the complainant requires.

Among the other tactics employed by Stitt and Limitone are challenging any agency's jurisdiction if the
complainant has communicated about the grievance with
any other federal or state agency and suggesting that
the second investigator contact his predecessors--here
the authors note that they "...have never had any difficulty with EEOC in this area."

Sometimes a complainant seeks an injunction to prevent the university from terminating her employment,
since she maintains that she will probably prevail on
the merits of the case and the injunction will prevent
irreparable injury. Stitt and Limitone here advise the
university to answer by demonstrating that the termination was due to financial stresses, departmental reorg-
anization, insubordination, a more qualified applicant,
or some such. The university should also, according to

29. R. S. Stitt and A. P. Limitone, Jr., "University Fair
Employment Practices Litigation Strategy and Tactics,"
Journal of College and University Law 1973:20-32.

these authors direct the court's attention to the complainant's right to termination benefits and unemployment insurance. They even state that the court should be reminded that if the complainant is successful she can be awarded back pay with no loss of seniority. This last is, of course, unreasonable for any academic person, but particularly when the complainant is a scientist who is operating a research project since terminating her can clearly cause irreparable injury in the laboratory and in obtaining and continuing her funding from outside agencies.

We hope that universities will change the direction in which their lawyers have been taking them. Universities' attorneys too often act like most other attorneys in that they do everything necessary to win the case for their clients, and they perceive their clients to be the administration of the universities rather than the community of scholars. It is surely the job of the faculty and staff to remind them who their clients really are and to prevent members of the administration from acting in all inhumane fashion.

The chair of the Faculty Senate of the University of Pennsylvania has recently written,

> As you know, last year the General
> Counsel took two controversial and
> erroneous positions regarding the
> meaning of the grievance procedures,
> and communicated these to grievants
> and their advisors. After these errors
> were corrected, I asked the President
> of the University to instruct the
> General Counsel not to involve him-
> self in pending grievances in the
> future or to purport to interpret
> the meaning of the faculty's griev-
> ance procedures. The President
> agreed to write such a letter to the
> General Counsel. Under our griev-
> ance procedures, questions of the
> interpretation of the procedures
> are to be resolved in the first
> instance by the Grievance Commission,
> with appellate review by the Senate
> Executive Committee. The Senate

> Committee on Academic Freedom also
> has an interest, when questions with-
> in the jurisdiction of that committee
> arise. In my view, it is harmful for
> the General Counsel, who represents
> the entire University, to take an
> adversarial role in an internal
> grievance and it is also harmful for
> him to seek to pre-empt the bodies who
> have responsibility for interpreting
> grievance rules should controversies
> about interpretation arise.[30]

One of the signs of a great university may well be
the resources it places at the service of women and
minorities.

RECENT PROGRESS

What is the current situation in academe as it bears
on the future of academic women? In the courts the recent
case of Sweeney v. Board of Trustees of Keene State College
was heard by the U.S. Court of Appeals, First Circuit
(Boston). Christine Sweeney won her case in the U.S.
District Court for New Hampshire, and the judgment was
affirmed on appeal on January 4, 1978. The district court
had found that Sweeney had been a victim of sex discrimination in her second effort to gain promotion, ordered her
promotion backdated to 1975 with the appropriate back pay,
and awarded legal fees. Senior circuit judge Tuttle said
that the judges were rejecting an effort by the defendants
"...to elevate the quantum of proof (of discriminatory
motivation) to such a level that a litigant is necessarily
doomed to failure." The judges voiced misgivings over
"...the notion that the courts should keep hands off the
salary, promotion, and hiring decisions of colleges and
universities." Citing their awareness that Congress has
evidenced a concern for the status of women in academia
they cautioned "...against permitting judicial deference

---

30. P. Bender, chair of Faculty Senate, University of
Pennsylvania, to R. E. Davies, chair of Senate Committee
on Academic Freedom and Responsibility, University of
Pennsylvania, October 27, 1980.

to result in judicial abdication of a responsibility
entrusted to the courts by Congress."[31]

Of great interest is the judges' acceptance of
statistical evidence that a double standard was applied
to promotion decisions. An important part of the case
was the evidence "...that the person who nominally served
as affirmative action coordinator did virtually nothing
to advance the rights of women on the Keene campus."
Many academic women will find that this statement has an
all too familiar ring. This case was the first in which
a court itself ruled on sex-related employment issues
specifically on the allegation that promotion to full
professorship had been denied because of gender. The
Supreme Court refused to consider this ruling. Sweeney
was given back pay and legal fees.

Two other major victories for women were granted
recently. At the University of Minnesota, in response
to a class action suit, the university agreed in an out-
of-court settlement to pay a hundred thousand dollars
in damages to Shyamala Rajender, a former untenured
chemistry professor. It further agreed that at least
two out of the next five persons hired for regular faculty positions in the chemistry department must be women.
It also consented to the creation of a review panel that
includes a representative of the court.[32] The other
victory was the Muhlenberg College case, in which the
United States Court of Appeals for the Third Circuit upheld a lower court decision that awarded tenure to a
physical education professor. This was the first such
ruling to date overturning a college's choice to deny
tenure.[33] Another hopeful sign is the recent out-of-court
settlement in the case of Lamphere v. Brown University
et al.[34]

31. Sweeney v. Board of Trustees of Keene State College,
16 FEP Cases 378-387 (1st Cir. 1978).

32. W. J. Broad, "Ending Sex Discrimination in Academia,"
Science 208 (1980):1120-22.

33. D. Kleiman, "Female Academics Show Gains in Combating
Sex Discrimination," New York Times, July 15, 1980.

34. A. Gorton and A. F. Wessen, "The Lamphere Settlement:
A Faculty View," Brown Alumni Monthly, November 1977:25-28,
37.

Universities are still concerned about the possibility that HEW will withhold, terminate, deny, or suspend their federal contracts. This can be done by the refusal of HEW's Office for Civil Rights to certify the university as a responsible contractor when there are allegations that there has been substantial deviation from a university's approved affirmative action plan. Despite numerous false alarms the situation appears no more hopeful than it ever did. In our view, redress of grievances will only come from the individual and concerted efforts of people who care about the concerns of women. As Solon said well over twenty-five hundred years ago, "Justice will be secure, only when those who are not injured are as indignant about injustice as those who are."[35]

Whereas the courts are to be avoided if possible, their existence together with the recent executive orders make it far more likely that internal grievance mechanisms will succeed--especially as more people's consciousness is being raised so they become more indignant about injustices.

DISCUSSION

Discrimination in Recruitment. Judith Vladeck added an additional example of discrimination against women: A young woman named Irene Lo Re had applied for a job at Chase Manhattan Bank. She received two letters in response to her application, in the same mail. The first, addressed to "I. Lo Re," began, "Dear Mr. Lo Re: Your credentials seem to be in order and your application suggests that your experience is what we need. Please make an appointment at once to be interviewed." The second letter, addressed to Miss Irene Lo Re, said "Dear Miss Lo Re: Sorry we have no openings for a person with your credentials...." She was the lead plaintiff in a successful class action suit against Chase Manhattan Bank.

Use of Citation Indexes. One participant asked if it was the intent of the Davieses to say that, in using citations as an indicator of the quality of one's research, they

---

35. J. C. Livingston, Fair Game? Inequality and Affirmative Action (San Francisco: Freeman, 1979).

recognized that they were using an indicator that was
already biased? Robert Davies responded that one had
to be cautious in using citation rates--a person's work
could be cited often just because it is wrong. There
are a number of other things, he noted, which have to
be taken into account in using citations. But we can
say, he went on that in the analysis of some thirty-
seven or so criteria, by a committee of the Women's Faculty Club at the University of Pennsylvania, the only
one that came out as guaranteed to be free from sex bias
was citation of papers by a relatively junior person who
was not yet internationally known; this was demonstrated
in the case of a particular woman whose articles were
signed with her initials rather than her given names.
This work would be assessed then, by the totality of
scholars, in a fair way. So it appears that citation
frequency seems to be one of the best ways of assessing
the impact of a paper on a given field. Just lining up
the papers or counting them or weighing them doesn't tell
you as much--have they had any effect? At the very top
levels, this may only tell you that some famous work
(such as the paper on a technique for measuring proteins
that has now had over fifty thousand citations) just described a very, very useful technique. A few papers on
techniques do get an extremely high rate of citation.
One has to look at the top end for those. At the bottom
end, if, say, a woman is told that a man has published
many more papers than she has, she can ask how many
times his papers have been cited. He has a problem if
his papers--no matter how numerous--haven't had much
effect. Citations thus do provide an objective measure,
providing one has advice on how to use the measure.

Regarding name styles for authors, Davies noted that
some journals, like the Journal of Physiology, used to
allow a woman to use her first name in styling her name
and require men to use initials only. Some women chose
to include their full names because they felt it made it
clear that women scientists were publishing; others chose
not to do it because they feared that, if people thought
the authors were women, they might not take as much notice
of the papers. "Times change," Robert Davies noted. "I
have the impression now that more women are wanting to
identify themselves as women to show what women can do.
While it is true, he said, that "Anonymous was probably
a woman," we should not necessarily want to carry on that
tradition.

57

Davies and Davies

A participant remarked that there is a woman at
Cornell who has published for some twenty-six years
jointly with her husband, but now says she will never
publish with him again. The man always gets the credit,
the woman says, even when the woman does 90 percent of
the work; even when these partners stand side by side at
a party, strangers will shake his hand and congratulate
him for his great work.

That can be a problem, Robert Davies acknowledged.
Efraim Racker, a Cornell scientist, had remarked that
the Davieses announced their marriage in Biochimica et
Biophysica Acta. They have published only three papers
together (about 1 percent of their total combined publications), he remarked, and each of these lists her
name before his.

One participant remarked that women could really help
one another by seeking out one another's work and making
a point of citing it. "This is a hazard of citation
analysis," Davies observed. "It can be misused." But,
he noted, it has been misused already. "I was a department chairman for twelve years or so and would receive
applications from people who enclosed papers in which
they had cited my work--sometimes it was clear that the
only reason they'd done so was to be able to say, "I
cited your important paper on this or that." Citation
analysis is very revealing but by no means foolproof.

Sexual Harassment. In answer to a question, Helen Davies
said that allegations of sexual harassment of students
have not fared well in the court. The most recent case
she knows of came about at Yale; it was thrown out because the plaintiffs were no longer students. Such delay,
she said, suggests that women who bring charges of sexual
harassment had better be freshmen--and patient.

Sandler said that, so far as she knew, only the Yale
case had gone to court--with that unfortunate result. But,
she said, there have been repercussions of charges brought
by students on individual campuses. In one case, a letter
of censure was issued at Harvard; a faculty member at the
University of California at Berkeley was suspended for one
quarter without pay; and a tenured member of the faculty
at the University of California at San Jose was fired.
This is an issue institutions are rapidly becoming aware
of, are very embarrassed about, and ready to take some
stands. Even though the women at Yale lost that case, the
issue has been raised. Other women--maybe even freshmen--

will be filing. This has shaken up the academic community.
Getting it out in the open should take care of about 80
percent of the problem, she said.

Robert Davies observed that the University of Pennsylvania has created a committee to help solve the problem of
sexual harassment. The committee has acted decisively,
he said, so that one does not have to be a "freshperson"
on that campus to expect some justice. The important thing,
he added, is to publicize the existence of the committee
and to make known its desire to receive evidence of harassment of students.

The formation of the committee on a campus really
scares the lecherous old professor types, he noted, and
improves the situation. It is difficult to deal with an
individual case when a woman declares that something or
other happened in a closed room and the man denies it.
But when it develops that this has happened on a number of
occasions with several different students, then the matter
can be moved on. At Penn the office of the ombudsman has
been very effective in resolving these problems; they have
not had to go to court. Sexual harassment, Davies pointed
out, is not always a case of young female harassed by old
male. Sometimes it is young female, young male; sometimes, female against female; male against male; female
against male, even. Even though there has not been
much publicity in the paper about cases that have been
resolved, the situation is improving, Davies said. In
the old days, incidents of this sort were seen as just
part of "being human."

Choosing a Neutral. In answer to a comment, Robert Davies
emphasized the importance of having neutral people control
the grievance procedure. That has been done on his campus,
as spelled out in their new procedures. The hearing panel
is composed of representatives of all types of persons
throughout the university--males, females, tenured persons,
nontenured persons, and so on. "So far as I know," Davies
said, "they have always come to what seems to me to be
proper judgments in disputes."

"The problem arises," he went on, "in universities
like mine where the administrators say that they are paid
to administer and that they cannot delegate the responsibility for making decisions on who should be tenured to
any other body. Who should make the final decision? Official arbitrators? federal judges? We are not convinced

that the type of people who serve as professional arbitrators are likely to be any more knowledgeable about the way a university works than federal judges are. The people who are likely to be most effective are the very small number of professors on a campus--even if it is as few as 5 percent--who care about these things. They can organize themselves and be part of the committee on academic freedom or whatever. A small group of concerned faculty can make a difference, Davies said.

A faculty member asked if the sex and race of the persons hearing cases were taken into account at Penn. Davies responded that discrimination on the basis of sex, race, and so on are, according to their procedures, grievable issues. The procedure, however, is blind to these issues, that is, it works the same way for all grievants. Grievants may choose an adviser--a law professor or anyone else--to assist them during the hearings. The panel from which persons are chosen to hear the cases must include women and minorities, Davies concluded, but this is not necessarily the case with the specific group chosen to hear a case. The group from which the specific group is chosen must be representative. It excludes administrators such as deans, department chairpersons, and vice provosts. Once the panel is chosen from the pool, then the grievant or the institution can challenge the inclusion of certain members if they feel that the specific group to hear a case is not appropriate. This challenge can be for cause or a peremptory challenge.

A minority faculty member stressed the importance of the final group members being sensitive to issues of discrimination on the basis of sex and race. Davies concurred. But, he noted, based on his seven years of association with grievance committees, that sometimes the worst antifeminists are women. Thus sensitivity on these matters is not dependent on a person's sex or race." The worst anti-Semitic remarks I've have ever heard," he said,"came from Jews, and the worst antiblack remarks have come from blacks. "

Helen Davies remarked that she had wanted a specification that the larger pool, from which hearing groups are chosen, must include a certain proportion of women and minorities. But that could not be included because so many faculty members had to approve the procedures on their campus. The procedures, as they stand now, are the best that could be done at the time, she said.

A faculty member inquired how the grievance procedure at the University of Pennsylvania works if the conflict is between an individual faculty member and his or her department. The cases the Davieses had described seemed to involve conflict between individual faculty and the central administration, whereas most grievances with which he is familiar focus on disputes between a faculty member and his or her colleagues. How does the arbitration process work if, for example, a faculty member is voted down for promotion in his department and he takes issue with the decision? If he has certain defenses that are technical—that have to do with the field—that he wants to make. How does it work then?

"The wording of our procedure," Davies advised, "reads, 'A grievance is a claim that action has been taken which involves the faculty member's personnel status or the terms or conditions of his or her employment which is arbitrary or capricious or which is discriminatory with regard to [the long list of factors] or not in compliance with university procedures or regulations.' Those are the grievable issues. There are of course other issues—such as those involving academic freedom, which are processed through another committee. There are a number of other judicial procedures that deal with other problems such as those brought about by a faculty member who throws rocks at the university buildings during a demonstration. The specific issue you raise—the one in which a faculty member grieves because his department won't promote him or give him a raise or where the department chairperson says, 'I don't think much of your research so we have changed your office to this broom closet'—those issues surely affect a faculty member's personnel status or the terms and conditions of employment. So that is grievable under our procedures. Another option a faculty member at Penn has is to go to the next level up. If a chairperson makes a decision one thinks is bad, one can go to the dean, one can appeal a dean's decision to the provost, and so on. A grievance therefore does not have to stay within the department unless the faculty member lets it stay there."

Thus, Robert Davies said, faculty members who feel that they were denied promotion because the department members don't know where the cutting edge of research is can take the grievance out of the department—and they can win. They can appeal to the dean or to the school's promotion

committee. The provost can move in on a department
and say, "You may not continue to operate this way."

Retribution. "We have heard from your paper," one
participant said to the Davieses, "that some faculty
members knowingly make false statements, forge documents, and so on. What happens to them? One reason
we have seen so little change," she said, "is that,
even if a woman does manage to win her case after
five years of struggle, the same men are still full
professors, are still chairmen of departments, and
are not one penny poorer than they were when they
violated university regulations."

     Robert Davies responded that that was provided for in
Section 6 of the procedure, and on the matter of tim-
ing, the procedure states the grievance must be completed within a year. "Typically, it has taken much,
much longer in the past," he noted, "usually because
the administration, for reasons it feels are very
good, has dragged its feet. The grievant is kept on
until the grievance is resolved, in our new procedures.
Even in the case of Sharon Johnson at the University
of Pittsburgh, there was a court injunction which kept
her at the university until the judge finally decided--
improperly, in my view--that her case had no merit."

     "If the grievance procedure uncovers an action
which seemingly violated University of Pennsylvania
procedures which resulted in a discriminatory action,
it is the responsibility of the presiding officer to
bring the matter to the attention of the Chairman of
the Senate and the Provost," Davies quoted. Working
through various channels, the matter must be investi-
gated before the end of another semester and a report
made. "There was a case," Davies said, "in which the
provost did not act in the way we felt was proper.
When mechanisms were instituted to bring him before
the Committee on Academic Freedom and before a court,
he resigned--an aroused faculty, working through proper
channels, can do very many of the things it wants to--
and at that same time our president resigned. So even
people as high as that can be dealt with. Trustees
are harder to deal with, but we are working on that."

     "In the case of Sharon Johnson," Davies reported,
"I was able to use the citation index to show--and nobody has ever controverted this--that her published

work was equal in quality to that of the full professors
in her department. The only man who was significantly
better was a member of the National Academy of Sciences.
She was as good or better than every other member of the
department. By our method, you can compare the citations
of senior people with those of junior people. The only
problem with it was that the judge said that, since that
method of measurement had just been invented, he could
not consider it a reliable method. Perhaps it will become more accepted with the passage of time. This
method of weighing citations is not perfect, but it
certainly is a better method than just counting publications."

Sensitivity to the Existence of Discrimination. One
participant remarked that even if members of the academic
community have good will in these matters, they sometimes
lack information about the extent to which there is discrimination against women at universities.

Helen Davies noted that she had been the faculty
colleague, that is, the adviser and spokeswoman, for the
first woman to win a grievance at the University of Pennsylvania. "What I did was lay out some of the social
research that has been done--the studies of Fidell,
Simpson, and so on. When you can show that 85 percent
of the time, males were chosen over females with identical credentials, then even people in the arts can be
persuaded! Numbers are radical in that when you provide
documentation--clear and unambiguous evidence that preju-
dice exists in higher education--then people tend to agree
not that they themselves could be biased but that their
colleagues could very well be."

Women's Network. Helen Davies read from the minutes of
the women's group at the University of Pennsylvania,
WEOUP: "The new officers will be installed...in the
Faculty Tearoom." "Congressman William Gray will install
the new officers." This information went on bulletin
boards around the campus--"WEOUP to hold meeting" and in
the minutes. "These are the most avidly read minutes
of any in the university," she said, "the administration
can't wait to get its copy and see 'what those damn women
are doing now.' Congressman Gray is a minority member--
he will be a good source of information for the group.
Our president is a minority woman. So we have these ties,

and a small amount of panic enters the administrative
bosom at the thought.

"Even the treasurer's report is interesting. It
is one of the few of its kind that is really read.
'WEOUP has $450 in its expense account and $600 in its
Legal Defense Fund....' A typical entry reads, 'It was
decided that this $600 will be used to provide counsel
for a woman professor. WEOUP has contributed $1,000
to the case. WEOUP is hopeful that the case will be
resolved at Penn. If not, WEOUP will begin a national
fundraising drive to support the case.' These are
important minutes. They are one of the mechanisms by
which WEOUP increases its effect. WEOUP is an organization, not just of faculty women, but of women all across
the university. The first president was a secretary.
To be sure, she had a protected position--she was
my husband's secretary--but she has gone to college,
earned her bachelor's degree, she is now in law school,
and she is the head of our women's center. We expect
to send her someday to Congress where she can do lots
of good things for all of us!

"This is the kind of networking I recommend, women
helping one another as individuals. Our mailing list
has seven thousand names--not all dues payers, to be
sure--but seven thousand people get our minutes. Nobody
in the whole university is safe from WEOUP, in a sense.
Some secretary who is typing up information about faculty
salaries may be sending a copy to WEOUP; nobody can be
sure. In fact, a good deal of our information has come
through these 'informal' channels. This is a radical
kind of networking; it gives our organization a kind of
leverage.

"WEOUP did send money and faculty representatives
to the University of Pittsburgh during the Sharon Johnson
case," Davies said. "The women there were terrorized.
We weren't; it wasn't our case. So we had nothing to
lose and could help. We sent a full professor to do
statistical analysis. This is the kind of interuniversity
networking we can do. The Philadelphia region has a very
strong network. We recommend this kind of organization
to you. It is essential for survival."

Robert Davies added that while the minutes of WEOUP
meetings are widely read now, it has not always been so.
At first, he said, it was practically impossible to keep
notices of any women's meetings up on public bulletin

boards. They were torn down within five minutes. Then the answer became clear. All the notices were posted in the women's rest rooms. They weren't torn down. If you are in an institution where the men don't want the uppity women to unite, you still do have places where you can communicate with one another.

Anybody who wishes to be on the mailing list, Helen Davies said, should get in touch with WEOUP.

4.
Strategies for Eliminating Sex Discrimination: Times that Try Men's Souls

Bernice R. Sandler

The word men in my subtitle, of course, clearly includes women as well. Of all the institutions in American society that have been criticized for poor treatment of women, higher education has been one of the most frequent targets. Perhaps this is because education holds out the implied promise of equality and equal opportunity. Women in education are especially angry because they have discovered that for them, the promise is broken. The myth of equality in higher education is just that, a myth. We have been told that education is a woman's field, and that the university is a place that rewards merit and talent. But we have also seen study after study that clearly indicates that women are still second-class citizens on the campus, even after ten years of affirmative action and federal legislation prohibiting sex discrimination. Nevertheless, much progress toward equality has been made in the last decade. Overt discrimination is indeed disappearing, but subtle forms that are far harder to identify and to prove, and far harder to deal with and to remedy, still remain.

Women are a new advocacy group--this is how we have to think of ourselves in the 1980s. We are questioning policies, questioning practices, and pressing for change. We are learning the politics of power. I want to talk today about the strategies and tactics, maybe more about tactics than strategies, that can be used to bring about change in higher education.

I am not going to discuss strategies for one's own survival and other kinds of strategies to speed an individual's upward mobility. I want to focus on strategies that can help us improve the lot of all women in academe--women as faculty, as staff, and as students. Let me say parenthetically that if you take on this task, you are not necessarily going to become tenured. Indeed, you may not be well liked or even respected for your efforts.

Whenever a group tries to change the status quo, it
antagonizes some people who cling to the present or the
past. In all likelihood, someone else is going to reap
the benefits of your hard work. The beneficiaries will
not only be your daughters, and in the long run your sons
too, but also some women who will probably not appreciate
or even know what you did. We have all met women, both
young and old, who believe that they became tenured or
were admitted to graduate school or became a Rhodes scholar
simply because they were very good, not because of anything the women's movement did. We have all heard asser-
tions like this: "I'm the first woman carpenter but I
don't believe in 'women's lib.'" Some women have absolutely no knowledge of the struggle that preceded them
and which made it possible for their merit to be rewarded.
However, as Helen Davies said this morning, give them
time. They will learn. I guarantee it.

If you want to be recognized for your good works,
and to be thanked, loved, and admired, women's work is
probably not the best way to do it. If women's work is
not for you, then much of what I have to say today will
be irrelevant. But let me ask two things of you: if
you cannot work with us, at least get out of the way--
and give some money to your favorite women's group.

FRAMEWORK FOR CHANGE

Let me put forth a general framework for change.
There are at least three basic ways to deal with problems
of sex discrimination. One is to develop strategies to
help women cope more effectively with problems of discrimination. These include providing internships, support
groups, mentors, assertiveness training, opportunities
for formal training in administration, and so on. These
are indeed very useful, but I shall not describe them here.
The second kind of strategy involves mechanisms for resolving grievances, which we heard about this morning from
Judith Vladeck and Helen and Robert Davies: litigation,
arbitration, mediation, and the development of institutional grievance procedures. These too are useful. The
third group of strategies are those that can be used to
bring about structural change in institutions. By that
I mean changes in policies, practices and procedures, and
the development of new programs that are helpful to women.
Most of these strategies are not very new or dramatic. Indeed, most of them are not going to solve most of the

problems we deal with. There is no magic answer that will
lead us to utopia. What I want to review today are the
strategies and tactics that have been used effectively in
other arenas. Thus this paper is not so much a plea for
new actions but suggestions for taking stock of what has
worked in the past and adapting and expanding that.

In resolving the difficulties women face in academe,
we have a fivefold task:

1. figure out what it is you want to change;
2. develop awareness about the nature of the
   problems that are involved;
3. propose specific solutions;
4. press for the adoption of these solutions;
   and
5. monitor the implementation of these solutions,
   whether they are policies, practices, or programs.

How do you decide what issue you want to work on? You
cannot work on everything. So, first, it should be something you care about, something you are willing to spend
energy and time on, freely. And second, it should be something specific that is amenable to solution. It has to
be particular policy, a particular procedure, a particular
program that you want. To end all discrimination is a
noble goal, but it is a lot easier to change a maternity
leave policy than to bring about equity for everyone.
Third, it should be the kind of issue that can draw the
support of other groups—other women's groups, student
organizations, unions, minority coalitions, or faculty
groups.

You will need to take on both long-term issues and
short-term issues. The latter are necessary to give you
and your group a feeling of success. If you take on only
long-term issues, it is very hard to know that you have
accomplished anything. The list of issues from which you
can choose is long, almost infinite: hiring procedures,
tenure, salary practices, part-time positions, flexitime,
fringe benefits, grievance procedures, union policies,
women as trustees, women as administrators, transfer
policies for students, degree requirements, athletics,
sexual harassment, child care, career ladders for clerical
staff members, equity in pensions, equal opportunity for
wives of graduate students or faculty members.

Once you have chosen the issue or issues you want to
work on, you will need to develop some awareness, among

women and men alike, about the implications of the specific issue. You may know that sexual harassment is a problem, but there are vast numbers of people in the academic community who do not even know what the term means and have never thought of it as a problem at their institution.

In general, we have to raise awareness. Specifically, we have to sharpen the discontent of women. If you are lying in bed and are comfortable, you won't bother to turn over. In order for change to occur, you must make people a little uncomfortable so that they will want to do something differently. We need to shake them up a bit.

Let me give you an example of raising awareness. Discrimination against women in education has existed for generations, from the days we first entered Oberlin over a hundred years ago, but it was only "discovered" about ten years ago. How did that discovery come about? In the early 1970s, WEAL (Women's Equity Action League) filed charges of sex discrimination against approximately two hundred and fifty colleges and universities. These charges led to congressional hearings on sex discrimination in education. At that time, the level of awareness was so low that not one member of the large educational establishment in Washington, D.C., would testify. "There is no sex discrimination on campus," they told congressional staff, "and besides it's not a problem."

Those congressional hearings, chaired by Representative Edith Green (Democrat, Oregon), began to open people's eyes. The hearings and the resulting publicity legitimized the issue. Sex discrimination began to be the subject of public and private debate and discussion, with legislation as the result. Thus we now have federal policy, laws that prohibit sex discrimination on campus and elsewhere. Sex discrimination became a legitimate issue.

Since that time, there has been a marked shift in the official responses from educational authorities. Nobody says, "There is no discrimination" anymore. Of course they don't say, "It is completely gone" either. They say, "Of course there is no problem with sex discrimination at my university, but it is still quite bad at Alternate State U—and terrible at Dismal Swamp College. Terrible." "At my college," they say, "we're taking care of it. Just stamping out the last tiny vestiges which may remain. Here and there." Just wisps. Call it lip service if you

like, but don't discount it. It is a start, an
acknowledgment that the problem exists at some level.
Sometimes lip service can even be followed by tokenism,
and that may perhaps be followed some day by genuine
movement toward equality.

STRATEGIES TO INCREASE AWARENESS

How do you develop increased awareness? A major
tactic is to document the problem and get the word out.
For example, in the early 1970s, women began to form
groups on many campuses and to press for a report on the
status of women at their institutions. It was an important
step because for the first time it came to public attention
that women were not as likely to earn tenure at universities as men were. It seems strange to us now, but that
problem was not even recognized then. Sociologist Alice
Rossi was one of the first to recognize the problem. She
counted the number of women holding faculty appointments
in sociology departments and compared their numbers at
each rank with those of men. She identified a pattern
that no one had really noticed before: the higher the
rank, the fewer the women. It was a remarkable discovery,
and it did serve to sharpen the discontent of many women.
At campus after campus, women analyzed their status in
individual departments and in the institution at large
and began to press for change.
Now is the time, it seems to me, to take stock and
begin the cycle again. The regents at the University of
Wisconsin have set up a task force to study their whole
state system to assess the extent of change there. It
is due to be issued soon; I think it will again help sensitize academics to the remaining problems of women on
campus. We have had ten years of affirmative action,
ten years of legislation. How much change has there
been? Many people would indeed be surprised to learn
how little change has come about.
Reports can identify specific problem areas and
also counteract the inaccurate but often widely accepted
notion that the problems of women in academe are essentially solved. All we have to do, it is said, is wait
for the women now in the system to make their way up
the academic ladder. True? False. But it will take

70

numbers, specific comparisons, and careful data
gathering to convince academics. Annual reports can
be helpful, if they are sufficiently specific. Large
institutions such as Cornell University usually have
an office to collect institutional data. We need to
be sure that they include data by sex. For example,
when they collect information about financial aid,
it should be presented by sex as well as by race and
national origin. These tabulations by sex, race, and
national origin are particularly important so that we
can trace the extent to which programs are helping
specific groups, such as black women, Hispanic women,
and native American women.

Other ways of increasing awareness include holding
campus hearings. This is particularly useful for issues
such as sexual harassment. Hearings in state legisla-
tures can also be effective. In California, women were
able to bring about hearings in the late 1970s that
served to sensitize academic administrators and other
concerned people on and off campus. Sometimes you can
get a sympathetic journalist either on your student
newspaper, in the local press, or in a national newspaper to write about specific problems or the general
condition of women on campus. Such publicity gets the
word out that there is a problem and that there are
people who care about it. (Incidentally, I am speaking
as though these events always come about in this sequence,
in a logical, orderly fashion. In real life, they don't.
These steps often blur together, and sometimes it seems
as though everything happens at once.)

Developing awareness and publicizing the problem is
not enough. Nothing is going to change unless you tell
people specifically how the situation ought to be changed.
So you have to come up with a specific proposed solution.
It might be a new grievance procedure or a new policy
prohibiting sexual harassment; it might be a fact sheet
distributed to freshmen during orientation, telling them
what sexual harassment is and isn't; it might be a new
way of improving recruiting outreach to women; it might
be a women's studies major. To develop your proposed
solution, try brainstorming with a group of people. Get
a group of people together and say, "If we could start
from scratch, what would be the best policy in that
particular area?"

You should always ask for more than you can get. No
matter what you ask for, it will be perceived as too much.

Whomever you are dealing with to try to bring about your
change will say, "These women want to change the whole
university!" Correct. We do. But we need to be prepared, at the same time, to compromise. Therefore, you
must ask for more than you can reasonably expect so that
you can compromise. For example, if you ask for just one
more tenured woman, the response might be, "She will have
to be part-time." So you have to leave some room for
compromise and keep some room for yourself. No administrator can capitulate entirely to your every request; you
have to leave room for an administrator to save face.
Since your request is going to be whittled down, you need
to be careful what you ask for initially. Then you can
be very "reasonable" in your compromising; you set the
stage for negotiating. We would do well to learn more
about such formal modes of negotiation as union bargaining. Many of those tactics will work well for women as
we become involved in negotiating for change.

When you have identified the problem, publicized it,
and developed an ideal solution, you have to figure out
who holds the power to actually implement the change.
Is it the chancellor? the dean? the department head?
the governor? the legislature? It makes little sense to
ask your department head to revise the policy on maternity
leave if that issue is the responsibility of somebody else.

Once you identify who has the power to make the change,
then you must ask yourself, Who are the people who can put
pressure on those decision makers? What kinds of pressure
are they subject to? Where and how can you exert pressure?
Publicity is helpful. Issuing reports and data can be useful. Other strategies include publicizing formal charges,
holding a press conference, writing letters to those in
power, writing letters to editors for publication, getting
alumni to write letters to presidents, to chancellors, to
trustees. All these actions give the impression of power
and give the impression that there is a lot of action going
on. The institution must respond in some way. As individuals and as groups, you can write letters to people who
may be able to influence the decision makers and to the
particular people who can effect the change you want. The
American Association of University Women (AAUW) has encouraged their members to write to the presidents of their
institutions and ask what the institution is doing for women
and to withhold contributions if the institution is not
treating women fairly.

Another strategy is to seek out tenured women, if you can find them, women like Alice Cook and Helen Davies, who can lend credibility to your cause. And enlist, if you can, the aid of sympathetic prestigious men like Robert Davies--also difficult to find. They can carry the message to other men on campus. This can be very important because sometimes men often listen better to each other than they listen to women.

Of course the major strategy is to have at least one organized group. Women are becoming quite good at creating groups. This movement probably has more ad hoc groups and caucuses than almost any other movement in the country. Although the women's movement is often criticized for being fragmented, its very strength lies in the enormous diversity of its groupings and the many targets they can focus on, particularly when working together on issues of mutual concern.

STRENGTHS AND STRATEGIES OF COALITIONS

It is a far better strategy to have lots of groups rather than just one. Groups can be categorized into three basic classes:

1. The outside group which has no campus connection whatsoever. That is usually a chapter of WEAL (Women's Equity Action League), NOW (National Organization for Women), a business and professional women's organization, or perhaps just a group that emerges in town. They can issue the most dramatic statements about the extent of the problems on campus because they are not vulnerable to retaliation. Of all the groups, they will appear to be the most "radical," which makes everybody else look "reasonable" and "sensible."

2. The on-campus group such as WEOUP (Women for Equal Opportunity at the University of Pennsylvania). This group acts as an in-house advocacy group. It raises issues and calls attention to the campus community to problems.

3. The official institutionalized group, typically the campus committee on women. This is most often the most conservative of the three. Usually appointed by the chancellor or president, its members have to be more conservative by virtue of their status as part of the institution.

In the best of worlds, and this happens on many campuses, there are people who help keep these groups together, and sometimes people who belong to more than one of these groups. In other situations, women

Sandler

cannot openly join both the campus committee on women and
a pressure group such as the local NOW or WEOUP. But the
members talk to one another; they meet for lunch; they
phone each other. For instance, the members of the inside group might say, "We're having trouble getting through
a new policy on maternity leave. Can you do anything?"
The outside group can then make some noise and say some
of the things that people on the inside cannot necessarily
say publicly.

As you press for solutions to be adopted, you un-
doubtedly will be involved sooner or later in coalitions.
That is a sound strategy: the formation of coalitions requires the cooperation of diverse groups. Often there is
a good deal of informal communication among these groups
and many overlapping memberships. Additionally, these
coalitions often go beyond women's groups. There are
numerous instances when women's groups have joined together
with black organizations and other minority groups to work
on issues of mutual concern.

Let me stress the importance of coalitions between
women's groups and minority groups. These coalitions are
critical if we are to avoid a split between minorities and
women. If we—women of all races and minority men—fight
among ourselves as to who gets the scraps on the floor, we
will never be free enough to ask for the places at the
table which are rightfully ours. A long-range viable
coalition between women and minorities in this country
would constitute a substantial majority: women, including
minority women, are about 51 percent of the population;
minority men comprise another 6 to 9 percent—depending on
how the Census Bureau counts them this time. Together,
then, women and minorities constitute 60 percent of the
population and could form a very powerful coalition. It
probably won't come for another five or ten years, but I
think it is coming. Women's groups have, from the start
of the new women's movement, taken a very active part in
pressing for the rights of minority women who suffer from
a double dose of discrimination.

Banding together as many groups as possible gives
the illusion, if not the reality, of power and purpose.
Part of the strategy is to look powerful whether you are
or not. It is often difficult for administrators to estimate just how powerful and influential women's groups are.
They simply do not know what standards to use. Sometimes
they will overestimate just how many women you represent,

and you can use that to your advantage. If you are short
of groups, you can create some, such as the "Ad Hoc
Council to End Sexual Harassment of Students," even if the
council has only one or two members. Within groups, you
can give people titles so that when there are letters to
be signed, the signatures can include a title of some sort,
such as "Chair of the Ad Hoc Council to End Sexual Harassment of Students." When I was at WEAL, I was chair of the
Action Committee for Federal Contract Compliance. In fact,
I was the whole committee. But it was far better to sign
a charge with the title than to just write, "Bernice
Sandler, Member."

Working with other groups and enlisting their help in
a variety of ways is extremely useful. Groups such as
WEAL, NOW, AAUW, Zonta, Altrusa, the American Civil Liberties Union, and business and professional women's clubs
are well worth getting in touch with. If they cannot
actively support you, they nevertheless may be able to
write a letter of inquiry asking for further information
about the issue at hand, such as "We are concerned about
the problem of sexual harassment on campus, and we are
wondering what the current status of the problem is at
your institution." These letters show that there are people
outside the institution who are concerned about on-campus
issues.

Incidentally, letters or requests for information
should typically be sent to the highest person possible.
It is better to send your letters directly to the president. He or she or someone in that office, at least, will
have to read that letter, even if it is then forwarded to
someone else in the institution for response. In Washington, D.C., women's organizations often send letters directly to the secretary of the department they are trying to
influence. The letters get put in a plastic folder; the
folders may make their way down through six or seven
offices where someone finally answers them. Copies of
the responses then go back into the plastic folder and
make their way back up through the channels. All up and
down the line, people are reading about the issue of sex
discrimination and getting a little more sensitized on
the issue.

Meetings with administrators to discuss problems and
to make recommendations are a key part of what happens.
In most instances, it is best to try to meet with the
highest person possible. Let me describe how one group

in Washington operates, the National Coalition for Women
and Girls in Education, which consists of between fifty
and sixty groups. It includes projects like the one I
direct, the Project on the Status and Education of Women,
but it also includes organizations such as Girls' Clubs,
Business and Professional Women, AAUW, League of Women
Voters, etc. In short, the membership list looks rather
conservative. We meet quite often with decision makers
in the federal government and prepare for those meetings
quite carefully. Beforehand, those persons who want to
attend the meeting itself come to what we call the "premeeting," where we hash out what it is that we are going
to ask for, what we are going to say, who is going to say
what, and which topic is to be assigned to whom. If
there is something we can't agree on at the premeeting,
we simply don't raise it at the meeting itself. That's
one of the rules we follow: at the meeting, we only
talk about those issues about which we agree.

One person is assigned to chair the meeting, to
introduce everybody, and to ensure that every topic gets
covered--to say, for instance, "We really need to move
on. Now Mary Smith wanted to say something on the final
guideline...." Somebody needs to make sure we are stay-
ing within our time and to make certain the meeting
runs smoothly. Any members of the coalition can participate at any meeting providing they come to the premeeting. If they do not attend the premeeting, they
can attend but not participate in the discussions. We
now have the reputation around Washington for having
very tightly organized meetings. These few rules have
been very helpful not only in giving the coalition a
reputation for being well-organized but also in making
our meetings more productive. If you are well-organized,
you are more likely to be viewed as powerful.

Another tactic used at meetings is to write a subsequent letter to those with whom we met, reminding them
what transpired and what they promised they would do. We
also try to have our team be greater in size than the size
of the team we are meeting with. If there are three of
them, it's good to have at least five or six of you. If
you don't have five or six to fill out your side, ask
your mother, your sister, a student, an intern to sit in
with you. That person shouldn't speak to the issues since
she wasn't at the premeeting, but she can take notes and
serve to provide support where it is needed.

Coalition members don't have to agree on everything. We work together only on those issues on which we share the same views. We work mainly on a consensus basis. If there are major issues on which we disagree--and that often happens--then we simply do not work on those issues as a coalition. When that happens, a few of the member groups may work on issues together but not as part of the coalition. The others respect their right to do that. We don't question one another's sincerity or commitment; we simply respect the differences.

This kind of cooperation is not uncommon, particularly in Washington, where we work with diverse kinds of people. Republican women and Democrat women have worked well together on a great number of women's issues. This does not mean that we have everybody's support on everything. We don't. But on those issues where the women in the two parties do agree, both on the Hill and elsewhere, they are able to work effectively together.

Another useful tactic to use at meetings is to ask for schedules. If somebody says, "Well, I'll get that information to you," then your response ought to be, "When do you think you can get it to us?" Often the response is "I can't say when." And then you must respond in turn, "How about two weeks from now?" Usually they then say, "Well, ah, er--," and you can say, "Well, how about three weeks?" Force them to agree to some sort of schedule, so that when the three-week period or the four-week period has passed, you can then go back. You check their office with a phone call, saying, "The information you promised us by last week hasn't come yet. We are anxious to meet with you again." Since, typically, they are not as anxious to meet with you as you are to meet with them, they'll get you the information faster than they otherwise would.

When you telephone someone to make an appointment for a meeting, he or she may respond that they are quite busy in the office right now. Can you phone again some other time? The way to handle that is to say, "I understand that you are busy this month, November. How about December 15?" When they say, "December 15? Well, I don't know" then you might have to say, "How about January?" Later you counter with February. There is no way that anybody's calendar can be full three months in advance. You have to press them for a meeting on a specific date.

If the decision makers reject your solution to the
problem you have uncovered, be sure to ask why and if
possible get their responses in writing. Sometimes it
is not only useful but surprising to see why your solution has been turned down. The reasons you believe are
the ones that are the cause of the rejection may not be
the ones that are cited. If you can get their specific
objections, and perhaps counter them, there is at least
the possibility of a compromise. Without the information
about why a proposal was turned down, you cannot fight
the decision effectively.

When you have been able to get the decision maker
to change his policies--it is almost always a he who has
the power to do this--your task still isn't complete because you have to begin the process of monitoring the
implementation to make sure that policies have really
changed, are being handled fairly, and are accomplishing
what they are supposed to do.

OTHER STRATEGY ISSUES

There are useful strategies that can be put to use off
campus as well, particularly within professional organizations. Sometimes there are two groups concerned with
women's rights in a professional organization. The first
is the official committee appointed by the powers that
be to consider problems of women in that particular discipline or profession. Second, there is often a women's
caucus or group within the organization, which members of
the organization can join and which also deal with problems
of discrimination. For example, the American Psychological
Association has both an official task force on the status
of women in psychology and an association of women psychologists. There are at least one hundred professional
organizations that have a women's committee or a women's
caucus or both. And these groups are very useful in
developing information about the status of women in that
discipline and disseminating information about all kinds
of issues involving women.

In some instances, these groups are evaluating curriculum, including textbooks. If women are to overcome the
handicaps of sexual stereotyping, curriculum revision is

critical. These groups are putting pressure on publishers to change the texts. At the same time, they are getting the word out to their colleagues that particular books are derogatory to women. If a professional women's caucus off campus says that such and such a book is inadequate because of stereotyping, the local campus group can use that information to good advantage in bringing about change they want.

Increasingly, women are asking that educational institutions be concerned with the problems of all women. They are asking their institutions to reach out to older women who want to return to school, to minority women, and other disadvantaged women who may need a special helping hand. They are asking that all institutional policies, practices, and programs be evaluated in terms of the way they affect women as women. This is what many campus women's committees are doing, and it is helpful in identifying problems and developing recommendations for change.

One of the strengths of the women's movement is that each woman and each women's group works on whatever issues seem most salient to them at the time. For some, employment discrimination is critical, and they define that as their major goal and activity. For others, changing the laws may be the first priority. For still others, providing female students with mentors might be the important issue. Those who wonder if integrating an all-male bar is an urgent priority are probably unaware of the legal implications involved in that kind of activity. Those who believe that the issue of substituting Ms. for Mrs. or Miss is frivolous have probably not grasped the social implications of how a woman's marital status affects the way in which people respond to her. Women's issues touch on almost every single human endeavor; there can be no first priority. We must let others set their own priorities for the issues they care about most. If they work on the issues they really care about, they will work hard.

When any issue affecting women arises, we need to raise it and deal with it, whether it is a major problem such as salaries or a small one like the use of the pronoun he in official documents. Every time a women's issue is raised is an opportunity to sensitize somebody. Sometimes that is the only result, just a bit of sensitization and growing awareness on the part of others. But it can be the first step in solving the problem—developing

awareness that there <u>is</u> a problem. We cannot win every
issue every time. Many times you can be sure that the
first time you raise an issue, you will lose. But the
second time and the third time, the chances of winning--
of bringing about the changes you want--are substantially
better because of the previous sensitization.

AGENDA FOR ACTION

The results of the 1980 elections were discouraging
to many feminists. In a democracy you cannot control an
election; in a democracy, sometimes you win and sometimes
you lose. We are going to need to rise to the challenge--
and it is going to be a challenge for many of us. Ad-
versity is supposedly good for one's character; we are
going to develop beautiful character. There may well be
crises ahead and dark days. But there is nothing like
a crisis to bring people together and get them moving.
We are going to see the development of new and stronger
coalitions. Blacks and Hispanics may get along better,
and I believe women, blacks, Hispanics, and other
minorities are also going to work together more effectively. There is much that we can do. We cannot afford
to waste too much time on despair.
We are probably going to have more trouble with
the new Senate than with the president. We will need
to "educate" and inform many representatives and senators.
So keep in mind that very few people are Neanderthals
on <u>every</u> issue. There are many legislators in Washington
who have outdated views on women's issues, who have never
once ever voted the way we wish they would on women's
issues. Yet every now and then, something touches one of
them, and he helps us. Senator Barry Goldwater is a good
example. He voted against the Equal Rights Amendment and
against other legislation that would help women. Yet he
did a good thing for women pilots who flew the planes during World War II from the factories to the airfields.
They were never considered veterans and thus never received any veterans' benefits, yet they were treated in
other respects as though they had been in the military.
Senator Goldwater became interested in that issue and
introduced a bill to grant them veterans' status. It
passed. So don't write off anyone.

Here in New York, you need to make your new senator aware that women's issues are important. He is a newly elected senator and is going to love being in that Senate. He is going to want to be elected again, and is going to have to learn to deal with you, his constituents. Wouldn't it be nice if he got some letters in the next few weeks from women? The letters could read, "Knowing of your great concern about women's issues and knowing about your sense of fairness and equity...." That kind of approach is helpful since few persons are openly and publicly against women. (Officials are often particularly careful in framing their public statements: "I am certainly for equity and justice but....") Ask your new senator if he will continue to support Title IX since that legislation has been so very important in getting rid of the quotas for women. He may not know anything about Title IX, so he might ask his staff to do some research. The staff members will then report to him on what Title IX is and what it isn't. Someone on the staff will then be a little more aware of these issues, and he or she may in turn sensitize the senator.

The point is that we cannot write off anyone we don't like. Maybe some senator or representative will be good on only one issue, and that will be because people like you took the time to write and call. There is someone in every congressional office who counts every letter that comes in. If you write early, before the legislator has even gone down to Washington, he may even see the letter himself. Therefore, I urge you as individuals and as members of groups to write your representatives and senators about Title IX, Title VII, or whatever other issues you are concerned about, so that they will know that people care about these matters and are watching what they do.

One strategy that might be helpful would be for a delegation of women from the many institutions in New York State to ask for a meeting with the New York delegation of the two senators and the representatives to talk about Title IX. The congressmen themselves might not come, but they would probably send staff members. Most legislators will be hearing a great deal from those opposed to the implementation of Title IX; they need to hear from the other side.

Another issue of concern has to do with the Equal Employment Opportunity Commission, which enforces Title

VII, the law that prohibits discrimination in employment,
including employment at universities like yours. The
current chair of that commission is Eleanor Holmes Norton.
She can remain on the commission until her term expires,
but there will be a new chair--probably a chairman. Right
now we should be writing to the president, urging that a
woman be appointed to replace Eleanor Holmes Norton and,
furthermore, that whoever is appointed be knowledgeable
and sympathetic to women. Nobody else will raise those
issues for us.

We need to seek out Republican women and make alli-
ances with them. Ann Armstrong, for example, has been
very close to the president. She played a major role in
the passage of the Equal Rights Amendment by the Congress
back in the early 1970s and is very committed to women's
issues. Many of us worked with her during the Nixon administration. She needs to know that we need her help
with Reagan on issues involving women; and she and others
need to know that they can count on us, in turn, to
support them when they press for women's issues.

We are a new advocacy group not only on the campus
but in the nation, and we are beginning to act like one.
We are making ourselves official by banding together in
groups with official-sounding committee names and individual titles. We are institutionalizing ourselves.
There are numerous women's programs in Washington, and
we may lose them if we do not put in the necessary work.
we are learning the ploys that other groups have used for
years, such as leaking information to the press, sending
delegations to the seats of power, enlisting other groups
to support our issues, and so on.

Perhaps what we are learning is the most fundamental
truth of all, that nothing changes unless someone does
something about it. If there is something we don't like--
and there is much that we don't like--we really have only
four choices. We can go elsewhere (although where you go
to avoid sex discrimination, I do not know); we can become
bitter or apathetic (indeed that happens to some of us); we
can knock everything down, destroy what we have, have the
revolution, and hope that something better arises from the
ashes; or, we can do what women and men of good will and
hope have done throughout the ages--chip away, bit by bit,
piece by piece, at the things that need changing. We know
what the long-range goals and the ideals are. We want a

society in which each individual is free to function to his or her maximum potential, free of the traditional stereotypes that limit the options of women and men alike. There is no quick, easy way to utopia other than boring away at it, inch by inch, working on the particular issues confronting each of us.

Let me offer a few bits of advice to those of you who will be working for change:

1. As long as you can get someone to change his or her behavior, don't get caught up in worrying about why they did it or if they truly are committed to women's issues. For my part, I really don't care why anybody does anything so long as they do the right thing.

2. Avoid paranoia at all costs, even when the paranoia is justified. If you begin to suspect someone of evil intentions, that he or she is plotting or whatever, check yourself by asking if there is an alternative explanation. Often there is. Many times things will happen because of incompetence and insensitivity and not because people are conspiring.

3. Remember that bearing the burden of second-class citizenship presents the unique challenge of making that burden an opportunity for growth rather than for bitterness and devastation. We in the women's movement are really like the little boy and the emperor's clothes: we can see the university for what it really is because we are not really part of it.

4. Watch what minority and other groups are doing, and learn from their successes and failures.

5. Keep a sense of humor because sometimes that will be the only thing that will keep you from weeping.

Sandler

The hardest thing about the women's movement is
that there is no real enemy to hate with self-righteous
indignation. It would be easier if there were. Men are
not the enemy, for surely many of them have been hurt,
perhaps in different ways, but hurt nevertheless by the
same rigid stereotypes that hurt women. Certainly we
need compassion for all those women and men who have
been crippled by their experiences in the past. We need
compassion for those women who act with an impatience
born out of bitterness and despair, for there but for
the grace of God go all of us. We need compassion for
those women who tell us that there is no discrimination
and who cannot yet help their sisters. We even need
compassion for those men who tell us that their wives
are "perfectly happy."

For all of us, what will be most difficult to change
are our own attitudes and assumptions about what women
want, what women are really like, what women need. We,
women and men alike, are going to have to work with women
in ways we have perhaps never done before, in full partner-
ship. In our society women and men have been trained to
relate to each other only as marriage partners, as lovers,
or in some sort of up-down relationship such as the male
boss and female subordinate. Yet the lives of women and
men are joined together inextricably. We cannot escape
each other, nor do we wish to do so. We are wife and
husband, mother and son, daughter and father, sister and
brother. The women's movement is not going to go away
because so many women care, and so many men care, too.

Society changes very slowly. All of us--women and
men alike--will need to help one another as we grope
together to work out the problems that arise as women's
traditional roles shift toward equality of opportunity.
It will not be easy. But no longer will women weep when
discrimination hurts. No longer will women grow bitter
because they are denied the opportunities that are the
birthright of their brothers. We have taken only the
very first step in a very long journey. I used to think
that five years would take care of the whole problem.
Now I believe it will take five hundred years--or more.

Let me close with a quotation which is said to have
been found on a tablet discovered by an all-woman team
of archeologists, assisted by women staff, and women
students:

And they shall beat their pots and pans
into printing presses
And weave their cloth into protest banners.
Nations of women shall lift up their voices
with nations of other women.
Neither shall they accept discrimination
anymore.

Now that may sound apocryphal but I suspect it may yet
prove to come from the Book of Prophets. For what women
are learning is the politics of change. The campus, the
nation, the world will never again be the same.

DISCUSSION

Ethics. One faculty member commented that representing
oneself as chair of a committee that existed only in the
imagination might give some people ethical problems.
Another faculty member commented that in a group just
getting underway, everybody who comes to the meetings
is an officer. Perhaps it is helpful to think of those
officers as speaking for a silent majority of women on
campus who are with you in spirit but afraid to speak out.
Sandler responded that that tactic did not exploit anybody, and therefore it did not trouble her; however, she
strongly urged those present to eschew tactics they feel
are unethical.

Helen Davies noted that the first time a person had
sent her confidential material not meant for her eyes,
she had agonized over the ethics of using that information.
Upon reflection, she had decided that it was within her
rights to use it. The material showed that another faculty
member had lied to her; she used it. "Perhaps I had made
the mistake of trying to be as polite about other people's
mail as my mother taught me to be," she said. "But I
realized that I should be playing the games my father
should have been teaching me all those years."

An attorney noted that bureaucracies rely on polite-
ness to make everything work. Going through channels
reinforces the status quo, but an unorthodox approach
makes the grievant uncomfortable and the people defending
the institution uncomfortable.

Sandler

The Tactic of Writing to the Top. An administrator ques-
tioned the wisdom of Sandler's counsel about writing
directly to the president of an institution. At her
college, she said, an administrative assistant opens the
president's mail and bucks it down to the appropriate
office for response. A person who persisted in writing
to the president would be labelled naive, she said.
Sandler responded that it would depend on the nature of
the letter as to whether it is inappropriate to send it
directly to the president. Obviously, it is important
to understand the way a system works before you try to
change it; people on campus are in the best position to
know what is appropriate. Letters from outside groups
most generally go to the president.

Sandler added that having several signatures on a
letter, particularly when they represent one or more
groups, is also helpful. An administrator from another
campus observed that her president is quite vulnerable
to letters from off-campus groups. Robert Davies added
that one way to keep a letter from being ignored is to
send carbon copies of it, and note that you are doing
so at the bottom of the letter, to other concerned
people, such as members of boards of trustees, deans,
and so forth.

Coalition Politics. One participant asked Sandler's
opinion on the wisdom of women's groups joining with
those concerned with the problem of hunger. Sandler observed that certain women's organizations, such as those
concerned with child care and women's health, should
surely find common ground with the hunger groups. But,
she said, those concerned with employment discrimination
will have more trouble finding an easy tie-in. It is not
necessary for cooperating groups to agree with one another
on every issue, she said. Women's groups should not, for
example, expect minority groups to be with them on everything.

There are no fewer than ten coalitions of women's
organizations in Washington at present, she said. The
oldest is the National Coalition for Women and Girls in
Education; others are one on women in the military;
one on pregnancy discrimination, now disbanded because its
goals were reached; one on women's health; one on the problems encountered by older women; and an appointments coalition. That one, she noted, is active at the beginning
of an administration; it will be busy soon.

Minority Women. An administrator noted that this was the
first conference she had ever attended at which minority
concerns and women's concerns were mentioned together.
The problems are different, she said. A black woman like
herself, she said, is pulled between her commitment to
civil rights and her commitment to women's issues. She
was sorry, she said, that there were few Hispanics and
black women at the conference.

Sandler responded that from the early 1970s women's
groups have been concerned with the special problems of
black women and other minority women. She mentioned
joint activities undertaken by women's groups and minority organizations. She related what happened in 1975
when the Title IX regulation was issued. It included
a proposed regulation which would have allowed HEW to
ignore many charges of discrimination. Groups representing Hispanics, minorities, the handicapped, and women all
joined to develop a combined strategy and eventually defeated that plan. Another example she pointed to concerned the Fair Labor Standards Act, which excluded
domestic workers. Minority groups had tried for years
to have domestics included in the coverage, but they
could not succeed until they were joined by the women's
organizations.

Sandler observed that minority women should take
part in women's organizations because "you cannot count
on us to know your issues as well as you do. And even
white women of good will sometimes honestly forget the
minority problems. They don't mean to but they do."

There is a myth that the minority woman is the
"golden woman" in academe, Sandler said. There are few
data on this question, but what evidence she had seen
has persuaded her that minority women are in fact worse
off in academic life than minority men are--and in more
trouble than white women are. One study showed that
minority women were less likely than either white women
or minority men to have appointments at the better known
colleges and universities. The myth that black women are
being especially wooed by universities and can essentially
write their own tickets is like the myth that all women
are especially advantaged in terms of faculty appointments,
she said. Individual women are seen as representatives of
their entire sex. A woman is made president of the University of Chicago and everyone says, "See? Women have
made it."

Prospects for Affirmative Action. One participant ques-
tioned the value of the strategies espoused by Sandler
by saying we should consider the results from affirmative
action programs small compared to the amount of energy
put into them. At the national level, what is needed is
an overall strategy that does not involve small, shifting
groups. We need the kind of organization and planning
that have made the Moral Majority the political force it
is, she said.

Sandler responded that, in fact, she herself had
underestimated the amount of hard work it takes to bring
about change. She reiterated that, with a new administration, there would indeed be changes in national programs. Members of the House and the Senate will want to
change things. There is clear danger of losing some of
the gains we have made, she noted.

But she reminded those present that a great deal of
progress has in fact been made in the last ten years.
"Ten years ago," she said, "faculty members were still
writing, 'Thank you for your application. You are very
well qualified for this post but we already have a woman
in this department.' Now, they may, in some instances,
still think it, but they are careful about saying it or
writing it down. There is much more awareness now than
there was earlier. And we have made enormous progress
in getting women into the professional schools. Before
1972, how many women did you have in the veterinary
college at Cornell or in the medical college or in the
law school?"

She observed that we might lose part of Title IX
in the years ahead, perhaps sports. But she predicted
that we would not lose all of Title IX. One participant
brought the news that a Continuing Committee of the
National Women's Conference was aiming to bring together
all the women's groups in the country to lay plans for
strategies to protect women's rights.

Focusing on the local level, a member of NOW spoke
for her group when she urged academic women to get involved in community organizations. "We want to support
you in your efforts on campus," she said, "but we need
your inspiration and your participation to be able to do
that." A male faculty member cautioned those present
that they must remember that this is a long process. "Who
will benefit?" he asked and answered his own question:
"Our grandchildren. How long will we be willing to stick
to this fight? As long as it takes. To eternity, if
necessary."

One national and local problem is that many women are not involved in the struggle yet, Sandler noted. For example, many women do not yet understand how the passage of the Equal Rights Amendment would strengthen families. Yet in her travels around the country, she finds woman after woman who says, "I'm not for 'Women's Lib' but...." and then gives a list of feminist concerns. Too many women still think of the general problem of women's inequities as completely unrelated to their individual problems. If we could only get them to see the connections, we could bring about change faster, she said.

A faculty member remarked that one hundred years ago, Elizabeth Cady Stanton was thinking about exactly the issues we talk about today. "I take hope," she concluded, "from the fact that there are people at this conference who were sent by their male vice presidents at their institutions. I think the kind of information we are exchanging should be made available to all presidents and vice presidents and administrators at all the colleges represented here." "And," she added, "the best part of this conference is that there are so many young people here who will carry on the work."

Sandler concluded by thanking those present for the tremendous amount of hard work they had done to bring about the new opportunities open today. There are problems ahead, she said, and there is much to be done. But "the future is in your hands."

5.
Progress and Pitfalls: Reports from Participating Institutions

The papers in Chapters 1 to 4 were presented on
Saturday, November 8, 1980. The next morning, participants gathered to share reports, observations, and
predictions. Some of the representatives had to leave
early, but left their reports to be read by others.
Others sent in reports to be read for them.

REPORTS

Princeton University. "Three things have happened
recently to change our situation. (1) In one year,
there has been a 50 percent increase in the number of
tenured women faculty. That is, in twelve years, the
university had found only nine women to promote to
tenured posts. In the last year, five more have made
it to tenure. (2) Previously, it had been said that
a women's studies program would have to prove itself
at Princeton before it could become a real part of
the university academic community. Many of us felt
it was Princeton that had to prove itself. Now, in
any case, a full-blown proposal for a women's studies
program has been developed. It will be voted on by
the faculty next month. (3) A faculty committee on
appointments and promotion policies has set itself
an ambitious and far-ranging agenda.

"The women named to tenured posts at Princeton
in the past have been, for the most part, on the
periphery of women's issues. Perhaps they had to be.
The new appointees are not, however. Overall, the
most promising of the three developments is the
third.

"Meantime, the Philadelphia Equal Employment Opportunity Commission has bogged down on the case of Diane Ruble, the assistant professor of psychology and well-known women's studies researcher who was denied tenure. Her situation has concerned many of us here deeply. We are approaching Washington, seeking action there."

Janet Martin
Associate Professor, Classics
Princeton University

Brown University. "We believe that our consent decree offers a model for the kinds of internal changes that are needed in order to increase the number of women on a faculty and to combat sex discrimination. I think a number of these could be initiated without a law suit. They include: (1) a set of goals and timetables for the hiring and tenuring of women; (2) a faculty committee to review appointments before they are made with the charge of assuring that there is no discrimination and that where a man and woman seem to be of equal qualifications, the woman is hired (affirmative action); (3) a set of clear standards and procedures for departments and for the administration for hiring, contract renewal, and tenure; and (4) a faculty-appointed grievance committee that would have the power to recommend remedies (such as hiring, renewing a contract, granting tenure) to the administration.

"Clearly the last is the hardest to achieve since most grievance procedures have no clout and end up merely asking the same individuals who made the earlier decision to reconsider. The advantage of a consent decree is that the woman grievant can go to court if dissatisfied with the committee decision. But even here we are having trouble, since our Affirmative Action Monitoring Commitee keeps getting overruled by the administration here."

Louise Lamphere
Associate Professor,
Anthropology
Brown University

Western Michigan University. "We have seen an increase from 21 percent women to 25 percent women on the faculty in the last five years. These figures include temporary, non-tenure-track appointees, however. The salary discrepancy

91

has changed from about 85 percent of men's average
salaries to about 95 percent average. An equity adjustment was made as a result of a union contract.

"A complaint filed with HEW in 1972 is still outstanding. It has been divided between the Department
of Education, which continues to handle the Title IX
portion, and the Office of Federal Contract Compliance
of the Department of Labor, which handles the affirmative action portion. On July 25, 1980, the solicitor
of labor filed an administrative complaint against
Western Michigan University for failure to produce an
acceptable affirmative action plan in compliance with
Executive Orders 11246 and 11375, indicating fourteen
areas of violation. This is, reportedly, the first
administrative complaint filed against a university.
WMU is currently involved in writing a new affirmative
action plan and has hired a professional firm in New
York City.

"Two court cases currently active against WMU
involve: (1) a tenure case in which the department
and dean recommended tenure while the chair and the
vice president denied it--the charge is sex discrimination, and the department is sociology; (2) a suspension case of an associate dean in the College of Health
and Human Services. The charges are sex discrimination
and handicap discrimination. The grievant was suspended
for refusing to provide medical records on the diagnosis
and prognosis of her disease, multiple sclerosis."

Patricia Klein
Assistant Professor
Social Sciences, College of
General Studies
Western Michigan University

Amherst College. "Our college first admitted women in
1976; the first faculty women were hired in 1974. We
now have 4 tenured women out of a total of 150 tenured
faculty. The effort seems to be not so much to retain
and promote the women faculty but to remain within the
letter of the law. One interesting development on our
campus is that there is now a critical mass of women
faculty and students who are, in fact, moving toward
acting together."

Ruth Stark
Assistant Professor, Chemistry
Amherst College

<u>George Washington University</u>. "A new affirmative action director has been hired."

<u>Ithaca College</u>. "Reportedly in the process of naming a new affirmative action officer who will have special responsibility for recruitment and promotion policies."

<u>Monroe Community College</u>. "This large community college was pressed two years ago to set up an affirmative action office. At present, the affirmative action officer is serving part time. He has an active affirmative action advisory board assisting him."

> Reported by Michal Montgomery
> Executive Director
> Office of Equal Opportunity
> Cornell University

<u>State University College at Cortland</u>. "Previously, we had separate athletic programs for women and men at SUNY Cortland; now the program is integrated. We have thirteen hundred majors in physical education. We have formed an athletic council of faculty, administrators, and students, both men and women. Our aim is to have a model program of compliance with Title IX."

> Marcia Spaeth
> Acting Dean, Professional
> Studies
> SUNY/Cortland

<u>State University College at Geneseo</u>. "We have a new president at SUNY Geneseo who is supportive of affirmative action. This is an enormous help. About a year ago, women lodged a complaint with my office that there was inadequate locker space for women in the field house. We have just completed renovations that made locker space equal for both sexes. This was financed out of our academic budget, which created quite a stir. We understand that HEW was so impressed by this that they are coming to investigate us. We have reached, and in some cases exceeded, our goals for hiring women. Among our new hires to academic posts, 49 percent were women. With regard to salary equity, we have rank-for-rank, women earning 99 percent of what men earn. However, when we compute the salaries another way, it can be seen that, overall, women earn only 80 percent of men's wages

due to the high number of men at the higher ranks. We
find it difficult to recruit women faculty in account-
ing and business; it is easier in fields like special
education. Women's studies is flourishing at SUNY/
Geneseo; we have twenty-three courses now; they have
among the highest enrollments in the college. We try
to encourage students (64 percent of whom are women)
to go into fields that are nontraditional for their
sex. We focus on outreach to rural women and mature
women who may never have considered going to college.
Part of our affirmative effort is to recruit men for
the undergraduate programs and women for the graduate
programs. About 39 percent of all employees are women,
and 29 percent of the faculty are women. At SUNY/
Geneseo we take special pride in the outreach, since
there appears to be a hunger for imaginative programs.
The institution was not so enthusiastic about our outreach until it became clear that there would be a flood
of applications resulting. Our women's center is now
open."

> Bette Adelman
> Affirmative Action Officer
> SUNY/Geneseo

University of Pennsylvania. "One problem affirmative
action officers on many campuses have is that they are
seen by women and minorities as part of the administration and by the administrators themselves as 'on the
other side.' One justification AA people can give for
asking for a more active role can be found in the Sweeney
v. Keene State decision. There, the judges reprimanded
the AA coordinator for lack of action on behalf of women.
Thus, an AA officer can tell faculty and administrators
that he or she does not wish to be liable in court for
AA violations.

"We have a new affirmative action coordinator at
the University of Pennsylvania. She has asked us to
have a conference just like this one on our campus!"

> Helen C. Davies
> Associate Professor,
> Microbiology
> School of Medicine
> University of Pennsylvania

University of Vermont. "We have a newly appointed
affirmative action officer; no formal women's studies

program but interest in it; a student body that is 50
percent women; and a comparatively large number of
women coming up for tenure next year."

> Joanna Rankin
> Assistant Professor
> Department of Physics
> University of Vermont

Loyola Marymount University. "In 1973, Loyola
(formerly a men's college) and Marymount (formerly a
women's college) merged; now there is a strong joint
commitment to women's rights. We have a high Chicano
constituency, an active committee on the status of
women, and although the women's center has been closed,
a women's studies program. Due to an institutional
commitment to human rights, we have an effective
grievance procedure that has in fact ruled in favor of
women grievants. Women are invited to serve on all
search committees; 50 percent of the students are
women; salaries of men and women are fairly close. On
the minus side, however, although we had the first woman
dean at a Jesuit university, she was fired peremptorily;
and there seems to be strong sentiment, even backlash,
against appointing women administrators."

> Reported by Virginia Merriam
> Visiting Professor, Genetics
> and Development
> Cornell University

Cornell University. "As chair of the Affirmative Action
Advisory Board, I take the group's mandate seriously:
we make policy recommendations to the provost and investi-
gate problems on our own initiative. Affirmative action
responsibility can't be thrown entirely on the administration; it must be shared by the faculty. In any case,
when AA procedures are violated, departments have the
liability, monetary and otherwise. A committee of
Cornell's Faculty Council of Representatives is reviewing the university's grievance procedures; the AAA Board
is monitoring their work. Monitoring recruitment and
promotion processes must be part of the ongoing procedures and not just a review of decisions after they
are made, it seems to me. I believe in the good faith
of the administration; the issue is to help them. There
is a $50,000 fund to encourage departments to hire women

and minorities--that is an example of an affirmative
action the administration has taken for which they get
little credit. In summary, we have a long way to go,
but we are moving."

Lee C. Lee
Associate Professor
Human Development and
Family Studies
Cornell University

Cornell University. "Two years ago, we had an Office
of Federal Contract Compliance review by Department of
Labor investigators, the results of which have not yet
been transmitted to us. We do know that the investigators
found here, as at other universities, the need for goals
and timetables. I can tell you that of seventy-nine
faculty hires last year, twenty-nine were women. That is
good, but I believe that the area of promotion to tenure
and the need for effective grievance procedures are the
critical areas at Cornell now. I believe the faculty
here must reconcile themselves to the fact that federal
and state investigators have the right to see personnel
files. We should not try to cover ourselves with the
shroud of confidentiality as at Berkeley. We are one of
eight institutions now being reviewed for compliance
with Title IX of the Education Amendments Act of 1972.
This much I can tell you now: the finding of that
compliance team will be based on very careful investigation of our athletics program. In recent years, we have
had several findings of "probable cause," that is, federal or state investigators have ruled that there is
probable cause to believe that sex discrimination took
place in individual cases."

Michael Montgomery
Executive Director,
Office of Equal Opportunity
Cornell University

Cornell University. "For another perspective on the
situation at Cornell, I shall speak for the Cornell Eleven.
It is difficult for us to rely on the good will of the
faculty or the administration at Cornell when women are
so underrepresented here. Of 765 full professors, only
34 (4 percent) are women; of 388 associate professors,
45 (12 percent) are women; of 355 assistant professors,

72 (20 percent) are women. Since 1971, the percentage
of tenured women has increased less than 1 percent.

"Twenty-two women have filed grievances against
Cornell with the human rights commission; of these, five
are named plaintiffs representing the group of grievants
known as the Cornell Eleven. We recognize that these
cases are hard to win, but we are determined to stick
it out--for fifteen years, if that is what it takes.
What remedies are we asking for? Tenure for those to
whom it was denied; tenure-track appointments for those
who have been unfairly shuttled into nonladder positions;
damages; the provision of sex equity education for administrators; and changes in the grievance procedure."

> Jacqueline Livingston
> Former Assistant Professor,
> Photography
> Cornell University
> Member, Cornell Eleven

Women Chemists Committee. "One of our major projects
has been to monitor the progress of women on chemistry
faculties. It is said that the number of women chemistry
professors has doubled in recent years. That is true.
We have ascertained that the percentage has risen from
1.5 percent to 3.1 percent--132 out of a total 4,253
faculty members at Ph.D.-granting institutions. The
biggest receivers and spenders of federal monies in
research and development grants, the top thirty universities, had in 1970 4 women out of 1,058 chemists; by
1978, 26 women out of a total of 1,009. Only one of
these institutions has ever been cited for noncompliance
with federal law. That was Harvard. The citation was
lifted after one day. I believe that these federal laws
are simply not being enforced. This suggests that the
law should either be changed or it should be obeyed.

"Ninety-five percent of the faculties with twenty
or more chemists have not one woman on the faculty. Where
we do find women, they are so often the only one--lone and
lonely. We have been urging departments to hire them
three at a time. Now, I may say, the University of Minnesota is going to have that opportunity.

"These prestigious chemistry departments granted
Ph.D.'s to 68 women last year, but only hired 7 of them
for faculty posts. Can it be that the women's degrees
are not as good as the men's? It seems unlikely. I
have observed that many department chairmen say they

just cannot find women chemists. But they seem to neglect looking in their own departments and in their colleagues' departments elsewhere, where they have no trouble locating male candidates.

"What is needed is more dialogue in a nonadversary situation. What we do not need is young professors marching off to jail in their academic robes. We cannot wait another three generations. One force for change can be the professional associations."

Wanda L. Brown
Chairwoman, 1976-80
Women Chemists Committee
American Chemical Society

DISCUSSION

These reports resulted in general discussion at the end of the conference. A faculty member observed that one way faculty members can help advance the cause of affirmative action outside their own campuses is in their role as reviewers for granting agencies. Grants could be held up, she said, if reviewers insisted that persons proposing research projects had to demonstrate their compliance with equal opportunity procedures.

On the problems of recruitment of women and minorities, a Cornell faculty member noted that her department chair persisted in believing that there are no qualified women in her field, despite solid evidence to the contrary. A faculty member from another institution noted that the best new-hire rate reported at the conference was under 50 percent. That is not good enough, he observed, if we are to make up for the past. It will be hundreds of years before faculties are equalized if the hiring rates are not better than that. At his institution, he noted, when a white male is to be hired, the search committee has to include the credentials of the two best women who were considered and the two best minorities who were considered. The result of this mechanism, he said, is that department chairmen must find women and minorities before they can declare their searches complete.

Grievance Procedures. In a discussion of effective grievance procedures, it was pointed out that special

attention must be paid to detail. Because procedures
outlast individual provosts and presidents, one cannot
rely on unwritten understandings. At Miami University
of Ohio, there is a superordinate committee reporting
to the president that reviews all promotion decisions
and sends them back if the proper procedures have not
been followed. The affirmative action officer sits on
that committee.

One tactic grievants can use is to insist that
their credentials be compared with those of white males
who have been promoted during the past three years.
Departments tend to talk a lot about how standards have
gone up and be unwilling to compare credentials fairly,
it was said. When women come up for tenure, there is
talk of great financial stress; the women may be turned
down and told that the reasons were financial, not related to their sex. But the next year, the institutions
mysteriously find money to promote a few men.

With an effective grievance procedure, the best situation, it was asserted, is the one in which the procedure
is never used because the administrative officers and faculty members are behaving honorably. The second-best is
the one that always results in the institution winning.
This means that the administrative officers were, in fact,
following procedures for employment decisions properly and
fairly. The worst situation is the one that always or nearly always results in the grievants winning. This means, it
was asserted, that new administrative officers are needed.

Confidentiality. The issue of confidentiality, and the
wisdom of going to prison to protect that principle, was
debated. It was noted that the concept of academic
freedom began as freedom of the students in German universities to travel about and study under whom they
would; it has come to mean the freedom to teach whatever
one deems best, but it should not be construed to mean
that one can do research on any subject one pleases.
Here, the example of germ warfare research was invoked;
this has no place in universities, it was said, because
such research cannot be published for the benefit of
the community of scholars.

Should Professor Dinnan at the University of Georgia
have gone to prison rather than reveal his vote? In the
opinion of those present, he should not have. The value
of accountability should take precedence over the value
of confidentiality. Academic freedom, one participant

noted, should not be interpreted to mean the freedom
to violate state and federal law nor the freedom from
prosecution for criminal acts.

Secrecy has not served universities well, one
participant declared. It was noted that the secret
ballot was developed to protect the rights of the powerless, so that they could vote away a tyrant in secrecy.
Now the secret ballot is being used by the powerful
against the weak. It is an uneven contest between an
allegedly unpromotable junior person and the massed
senior staff.

Another participant remarked that some faculty
members may be clinging to confidentiality for fear of
being held liable for slander or libel. A clarifica-
tion of the legal status of an opinion honestly given
would help relieve this unease, she felt. Another
faculty member present observed that the Dinnan
imbroglio had prompted her department's decision to
not write down any reasons for personnel decisions.
To which another participant responded, "Faculty members
should realize that any decision they make may have to
be defended in court."

At the University of Pennsylvania, Robert Davies
reported, one woman's dossier was subpoenaed by the
court and later published. The outrageous things people
had said about her were made public. She is now the
chair of an influential committee; she can look anybody
in the eye. "I don't think we need to fear disclosure
so much," he said. "Faculty members live together the
way people live together in families. Bad things happen,
but they are forgotten, and we go forward."

In that spirit, another participant asked if these
problems were really an issue of gender. "Isn't this a
classic case of the ins versus the outs?" she asked. "I
think we should ask ourselves how we--the women and
minorities--would be acting if we were the ins and white
men were the outs."

A more immediate problem, another participant said,
is that women and minorities are standing on a platform
that can be jerked away at any moment. Michael Montgomery,
executive director of Cornell's Equal Opportunity office,
concurred. "The legal protection of women and minorities
in academic life does rest on Title VII and on the executive orders," he said. "The orders may be changed with a
new executive in power. The only way everybody's rights

can be protected is by a strong coalition of women and men, minorities and nonminorities."

The reports from individual colleges made clear that some institutions are taking action to comply with both the spirit and the letter of the equal opportunity laws. Princeton doubled the number of tenured women faculty in recent years; Brown settled with its grievants out of court; SUNY/Cortland is striving to set up a model of voluntary compliance with Title IX; SUNY/Geneseo is experimenting with imaginative outreach programs; MIT is building in supports for junior faculty; the University of Pennsylvania made sweeping reforms in its grievance procedures.

And Cornell? Cornell University has had women students for more than a century and women faculty since 1911. Cornell offered the first interdisciplinary course for credit on women at any major university and founded the first women's studies program. Nearly a century ago, founder Ezra Cornell wrote that his university wanted and needed the best professors available "regardless of sex, religion, politics, nationality, or color." In November 1980, Cornell University had a conference. Ezra Cornell's great-great-great-great granddaughter (now one year old) was among those present. Many of us who care about universities and about the welfare of individuals within them left the conference with the conviction that discussions like those we had heard would ultimately make possible the realization of her ancestor's ideals--and the people of her generation, and her descendants, would benefit.

Appendixes

APPENDIX A

GO FIND YOURSELF A MENTOR

by Mary P. Rowe

One of my major pieces of advice for all women in
nontraditional environments is to find themselves mentors.
A mentor can be any race or sex or age. You do not have
to like him or her; therefore, you have a very wide range
of people to choose from, including both pleasant people
and those you consider to be dinosaurs. Anyone can help
you so long as this person is competent and responsible.

Often young people are told to find role models,
preferably of the same sex and same race, likable ones,
ideally of the same sexual orientation and value structure.
One is told to find this saint and then learn to be like
her or him. Saints however are few (especially ones of
the same sex, same race). Therefore, it is easier to find
a mentor. Even a dinosaur can be encouraged to be a mentor,
just so long as she or he is competent.

A mentor is a person who comments on your work, criti-
cizing errors and praising excellence. This person sets
high standards and teaches you to set and meet your own
high standards. A mentor teaches you how The System works.
If you are in a hospital or in industry, you learn the
organization chart and also how the place really works.
If you are in academe, you learn the organization chart
and also how the place really works. Most important,
you learn how to succeed in your studies, how to succeed
in your work, how to get promoted, on the basis of excellent work.

Mentors teach you which intellectual problems are
important and how to recognize them yourself. They
apprentice you in proposal writing, conference presentation,

This paper, not delivered at the conference, is presented
frequently by the author to women's groups.--Editor.

resumé construction. They introduce you to important
networks, talk about your work to others, and find you
jobs. Initially, they are your evaluators and the
links to other evaluators. They teach you how to set
your own goals, how to evaluate yourself realistically,
and how to succeed.

Many women find it hard to acquire a mentor. Senior
women are exhausted and occasionally jealous of their
uniqueness. Senior men sometimes ignore women, or they
advance on women as sex objects, or they avoid women
because they are sex objects and wives would complain.
Junior women are often shy. What can junior women do
to find a mentor, even if they feel shy?

Nearly any competent and honorable person can be
helped to become your mentor. I mean this, of course,
not in the Machiavellian, exploitative sense, but in
the context of respectful, honest behavior on your part.
Take responsibility for finding decent mentors.

First you need to observe carefully what kind of
person you are dealing with. Be receptive to advice
and counsel offered to you from responsible people even
if you do not particularly like them. Stay away from
people who want to use you or hurt you, even if you are
attracted to them. Because negative or destructive
mentorship is also possible, it is especially important
never to engage emotionally with someone who may wish
to hurt you. Do not pick fights or respond to provoca-
tion from negative mentors. Stay away from such people.

When you find honorable people who know more than
you in any important arena, seek them out. Be both
receptive and responsive. You do not want to use other
people yourself; the reward to others from helping you
lies in your own responsiveness and creativity. Thank
others for any help you get, give credit with scrupulous
care to those who help, bring credit to your mentors for
having sponsored you. Here are some possible steps:

> 1. Introduce yourself; make the first
> contact--always on a professional subject.
> Go up after class, write a letter to an
> expert, asking an important question;
> comment on his or her last article; send
> your articles in draft to her or him for
> comment.

2. Do it again, respectfully and intelligently.

3. Begin to ask for help about your errors and excellence. Cherish the good advice you are given, and thank your mentor when he or she is helpful. Say it even if she or he brushes it off or says, "it was nothing." Be sure you acknowledge all the help you are given.

4. See if you can apprentice yourself, as a research helper, teaching assistant, junior collaborator, proposal writer.

5. As you get to know your mentor, be friendly, open, and very professional. Get to know her or his spouse; introduce your own friends. Avoid sex with a mentor at all costs--unless you plan marriage or unless your professional work is so good that nothing can hurt you. If, however, sex does become part of the relationship, keep yourself visibly and sturdily independent. If a lot of work is accomplished, make sure you get credit for it. Try to be independent enough to move to another job or another city to advance if that becomes necessary.

6. Seek out several mentors if it seems at all appropriate. Nobody is or can be perfect at everything. You may learn different things from different people.

7. Do whatever you can to help your mentors forever after, and give credit in public for the help you've gotten. This reinforces good behavior everywhere. It will encourage you to become a first-rate mentor. (With care and practice you may even become a good role model for mentors!)

APPENDIX B

FACULTY GRIEVANCE PROCEDURE,
UNIVERSITY OF PENNSYLVANIA

I. Applicability

a. This grievance procedure shall be available
to any member of the University faculty, whether
tenured or untenured, whether full time or part
time.

b. A grievance is a claim that action has been
taken which involves the faculty member's personnel
status or the terms or conditions of his/her
employment and which is: (1) arbitrary and
capricious; (2) discriminatory with regard to
race, color, sex, sexual or affectional preference,
age, religion, national or ethnic origin or physical handicap; or (3) not in compliance with University procedures or regulations, whether or
not (1), (2) or (3) determined the outcome.

II. Faculty Grievance Commission

a. There shall be a Faculty Grievance Commission
(the commission) composed of three members of
the standing faculty with the rank of full professor.
They shall be appointed by the Senate Advisory
Committee for staggered three-year terms expiring
September 30. These three members shall serve
serially as chair-elect, chair and past-chair of
the commission.[1]

Copies of this procedure are available from the Office of
the Secretary, 112 College Hall, University of Pennsylvania,
Philadelphia, Pennslyvania 19104.

b. The chair of the commission shall be the primary administrator of the Faculty Grievance Procedure. The past-chair shall serve as presiding officer at grievance hearings. The chair-elect will observe the functions of the commission and may attend hearings. Each member of the commission may substitute for another member when necessary by virtue of a conflict of interest or otherwise.

c. There shall be an independent legal officer to assist the commission in its operations. The legal officer's appointment and terms of employment shall be jointly determined by the chairman of the Senate and the provost. Once appointed, the legal officer's professional responsibility shall be to the Senate.

III. Preliminary Procedures

a. Before filing a grievance with the commission a faculty member is encouraged to review his/her complaint with his/her department chair, dean, the chair of the commission, the University ombudsman and other University groups concerned with the protection of the rights of faculty members[2] in an attempt to effect an equitable resolution. Consistent with the informal nature of the discussions at this stage, neither a written statement of the complaint nor a written answer thereto need be prepared.

b. Failing to receive satisfaction, or not willing to proceed informally, the faculty member may take steps to formalize the complaint. He/she shall inform his/her dean in writing of the nature of the complaint and of his/her intention to file a grievance with the commission. Additional discussions will normally ensue, perhaps for several weeks. However, the faculty member may, after the expiration of one week from the date of written notification, request in writing a written statement from the dean of the reasons for the actions which

are the subject of the faculty member's
complaint. The dean's written statement
should either be approved by or accompanied
by the separate statements of the department chair and the chair of any departmental or school personnel panels which have
reviewed the case. The dean's and related
written statements should be supplied to
the faculty member within two weeks after
receipt by the dean of the written request
for such statements. Exceptions to these
deadlines may be necessary during the
summer months.

c. If the faculty member is not satisfied
with the outcome of the oral and written
exchange with his/her dean, he/she may file
a grievance with the commission one week
after the dean's and related written statements were due or received. Written notice
of the grievance and request for a hearing
shall be submitted to the commission through
its chair with a copy to the provost. Where
a faculty member has not filed a grievance
with the commission within 90 days of the
date on which the dean sent the written
statements of reasons, the dean may inquire
in writing whether he/she intends to file a
grievance. In that event, the grievance shall
be treated as abandoned unless it is filed
within 30 days of such inquiry.

d. Since grievances may be cumulative and a
faculty member may be uncertain whether he
or she has been aggrieved until additional
observations are taken, several years may
sometimes expire before the faculty member
is convinced or aware that cause exists to
set the grievance machinery in motion. In
consideration of this, a faculty member
may base his/her grievance on prior as
well as current events or conditions.
Since problems of assembling and assessing
evidence become more severe, however, as
time passes, the grievance, where feasible,
should be focused on recent or continuing
events or conditions.

e. In the event it should appear to the chair of the commission that the grievance raises a matter of academic freedom, he/she shall refer the notice of grievance to the Senate Committee on Academic Freedom and Responsibility (Senate committee) which shall promptly determine whether the grievance is in fact within the jurisdiction of the appropriate school committee on academic freedom and responsibility. In the event that a determination is required as to whether the grievant presently does or does not have tenure, the chair shall refer the issue to the Senate committee for determination.

f. The chair may determine that a grievance shall not be processed either because the claim is deemed not to be a grievance as defined in section I:b, because the matter at issue in the grievance has been the subject of a prior grievance or because, in the opinion of this officer, the grievance is of so little consequence or merit that no panel should be created. This decision may be overruled by the chair-elect on appeal by the grievant.

IV. Participants

a. Upon the formal filing of a grievance, the chair shall so inform the provost and proceed to the constitution of a hearing panel (the panel) in accordance with the procedures set forth below:
(1) The panel will ordinarily be composed of three faculty members chosen from a hearings list. The hearings list will consist of at least 20 persons selected by the Senate Advisory Committee from members of the standing and associated faculty. The list should be broadly representative (including women and members of

minority groups) but shall not include
faculty members holding administrative
appointments such as department chair,
assistant or associate dean and vice-
provost. Members shall serve for
three-year terms expiring September
30 of the third year. Appointments
shall be arranged so that the terms
of approximately one-third of the
members shall expire each year.
Replacements shall be selected by
the Senate Advisory Committee as
needed.

(2) The three members of the panel
shall be chosen at random from the
hearings list. The grievant and the
respondent (see paragraph b below)
may each exercise up to three peremptory challenges. The commission, on
its own motion or on the motion of
the grievant or the respondent, may
disqualify individuals on the hearings
list for service on a particular panel
for reasons such as family or other
potentially biasing relationships to
either the grievant or others in
volved in the case or prior involvement in voting or other actions
bearing upon the case, or membership in the same department as the
grievant. The commission will devise
rules for the random selection of
panel members.[3]

b. The chair of the commission shall ask the
provost to designate the University person
(the respondent) who shall act on behalf of
the person or persons taking the action
complained of.[4]

c. The grievant may have a University
colleague aid in the preparation and
presentation of his or her case to the
panel. Such a colleague should normally
have academic qualifications in the
grievant's field of study and therefore
be able to provide expert assistance in

the case. When the grievant has the aid
of a colleague, the corresponding opportunity will be extended to the respondent.
The University colleague for the respondent
shall, however, be in that category of persons eligible to serve on panels. It is
not the intention of these provisions to
permit either party to have such a University colleague serve as legal advocate in
the presentation of the case.

d. The chair shall ascertain whether the
grievant chooses to have a University
colleague and, if so, whether the respondent
also chooses to have a University colleague.
The chair shall convey to the presiding officer the written notice of the grievance
and the names of the panel, the respondent
and the University colleague(s), if any.[5]

V. Procedures

a. The decision on the merits of a grievance
will be made by the panel after hearings in
which the grievant and the respondent have
the opportunity to present their cases.
Hearings shall be chaired by the presiding
officer, assisted by the legal officer.
Arguments, oral and documentary evidence
and witnesses will be presented first by
the grievant and then by the respondent.
The presiding officer shall have the power
to call witnesses and to introduce documents and shall, at the request of the
panel, obtain expert opinion from inside
or outside the University. Each side
shall have the right to address questions
through the presiding officer to witnesses
introduced by the other side. If panel
members then have questions, they may sub-
mit them in writing to the presiding
officer.[6]

b. A hearing will follow an agenda prepared
by the legal officer that is based on
prior demonstration of relevance by the
grievant or the respondent. Such determinations

of the relevance of issues, oral statements
or other evidence by the legal officer
may be overruled by the presiding officer
on appeal by a party.

c. The legal officer and the presiding
officer shall have access to all documentary evidence that is in the custody
or under the control of the person or
persons who took the action complained of
or of the grievant and that is deemed by
those officers to be relevant to the
grievance.[7] If documentary evidence is
needed by the grievant or the respondent
in the preparation of his or her case,
or by the panel in the course of its
deliberations, application for access to
such evidence shall be made to the legal
officer, who shall determine, subject to
appeal to the presiding officer, whether
the evidence requested is relevant and,
under the authority of the commission,
shall obtain evidence deemed relevant.
All such evidence shall be available
to the panel, the respondent, the University colleague(s), if any, and subject
to restrictions of confidentiality, to
the grievant.[8]

d. The commission may establish such
further rules and procedures as it deems
necessary to supplement those specified
herein. Where procedures have not yet
been adopted, the presiding officer may
rule on the matter. Appeals from such
rulings may be brought to the other members of the commission and, if denied,
to the Senate Advisory Committee.
Appeals from rules established by the
commission may also be presented to the
Senate Advisory Committee. Procedures
adopted under this provision should be
included in the annual report of the
commission. (see section X.)

111

Appendix B

VI. Findings

a. The panel shall prepare a written report
which may include a minority opinion. After
making its decision but before writing its
final report, the panel shall discuss with
the legal officer and/or the presiding
officer the most appropriate way to present
its report. The report shall contain a
clear statement of the elements of the
grievance and the panel's decision with
respect to each one. In cases in which
any element of the grievant's claim is upheld, the salient findings of facts that
have led the panel to each of its conclusions with respect to the injury done
to the grievant shall be summarized. The
panel may propose remedies. The panel shall
not however have the responsibility or the
authority to make a reevaluation of professional competence. In cases involving
appointment, promotion or tenure it may
recommend a full review and reevaluation
of the case. The panel may suggest to the
provost procedures that might be followed
in such a reevaluation, but the choice of
procedures remains with the provost. The
provost shall ensure that the recommendations of the panel and its supporting documentation, if any, are included in the
documents considered in the reevaluation.

b. The presiding officer shall distribute
the panel's report to the grievant, the
provost and the respondent. The person
or persons who took the action complained
of may obtain copies of the report from
the commission chair or the provost.

c. Since the panel's report is to be
succinct, the provost may wish to con-
sult with the presiding officer to obtain
more information about the case. It
shall be the duty of that officer to provide the provost, upon request, with the
details underlying the panel's report
and to make available the full documentation.

d. While the panel's report is to be accorded great weight, it is advisory to and not binding upon the provost. The provost's decision shall be made and communicated in writing within six weeks to the chair of the commission, the grievant and the respondent. In the event the provost declines to implement the recommendations, the written communication shall include the detailed reasons, and shall be sent also to the chairman of the Senate.

e. When the presiding officer is satisfied that the final action on the case within the University has been taken, he/she shall recommend to the chair of the commission that the panel be dissolved.[9]

f. If the grievance proceeding uncovers an administrative action or practice that seemingly violated University procedures or otherwise led to inequitable treatment, it is the responsibility of the presiding officer to bring the matter to the attention of the chairman of the Senate and the provost. The chairman of the Senate, working through the ombudsman, the Senate Committee on Academic Freedom and Responsibility or other channels, should see to it that the matter is examined. The chairman of the Senate shall report to the Senate Advisory Committee not later than the following semester whether such actions or practices have been found to exist and if so what measures have been taken to correct them.

VII. Confidentiality

a. Since the work of the commission and its panels requires the highest level of sensitivity to the privacy of all concerned, members of the commission, members of panels, grievants, respondents, University colleagues and witnesses shall accept the moral obligation to maintain confidentiality with respect to oral and documentary evidence presented

and deliberations occurring during the
processing of individual cases (except
as necessary in the preparation of a
case or as otherwise noted in this
document). All others are expected
to respect the privacy of all concerned
to the greatest extent possible.

b. Except as otherwise provided in this
document, or as authorized by the chairman of the Senate, the report of a panel
shall be treated as confidential by all
participants in a grievance proceeding
and by all members of the University community.

VIII. Hearing by the Senate Committee on Academic
Freedom and Responsibility

a. In cases which involve reappointment,
promotion or tenure, and in which the provost has declined or failed to implement
the recommendations of the panel to the
satisfaction of the grievant, the grievant
may obtain a hearing before the Senate
Committee on Academic Freedom and Responsibility (Senate committee) on the actions
of the provost. The report and recommendations of the panel and the statement of the
provost shall then be made available to the
committee. The committee shall also have
access to all evidence presented to the
panel and the records of the hearing before
the panel.

b. The Senate committee shall follow as
far as possible procedures consistent with
section V:a for the conduct of the hearing.
The parties shall not be permitted to
introduce evidence presented before the
panel, and the findings of fact of the panel
shall be accepted by the Senate committee
if they seem to have been fairly arrived
at. The Senate committee shall determine
whether the provost's action in declining
or failing to implement the recommendation of the panel to the satisfaction of

the grievant was reasonable in the circumstances. If the Senate committee finds that there is significant evidence that was not previously available to the party asserting its relevance, it may return the case to the presiding officer for consideration by the panel.

c. The Senate committee shall promptly report its findings and recommendations to the president with copies to the provost, the chair of the commission, the panel, the grievant and the respondent. A copy shall also be given to the editor of _Almanac_.

IX. Expenses

Necessary and proper expenses for processing a grievance shall be met from University resources. It shall be the responsibility of the presiding officer to determine what is necessary and proper. To the extent possible, administrative and secretarial services should be provided by the office of the Senate. Services that cannot be furnished in this way and other necessary costs should be charged to a commission budget in the office of the Senate. These charges shall be under the administration of the chair of the grievance commission.

X. Annual Report

An annual report should be written by the commission at the end of the academic year. It should describe the activities of the commission and give an account of the cases completed or in progress with due regard for the maintenance of confidentiality. It should be sent to _Almanac_, the chairman of the Faculty Senate, the president and the provost.

Notes

1. The cost of compensatory release from teaching should be provided from central University funds as needed.

2. The chair of the commission shall invite such University groups to identify themselves.

3. The designation of panel members shall be made according to the random order except that no member of the hearings list who has already served on a panel shall be designated for service on further panels until all eligible members have served at least once. These panel members, where possible, shall continue to serve on the panel until the case is concluded, even if this means that they serve beyond the time they retire from normal service on the hearings list.

4. Such "person or persons who took the action complained of" might include the following: department chairpersons, department personnel committees, department members who decide on departmental recommendation for personnel action, the deans of the schools, the school personnel committees, the faculties of the school, the provost and the president.

5. This process should be completed within four weeks of the date of filing the grievance.

6. There must be a majority of the panel present at all times during all hearings. It is the responsibility of the grievant and the respondent to ensure the presence of their witnesses at times deemed appropriate by the legal officer. Neither the grievant nor the respondent may present evidence to the panel unless the other is present. One and only one tape recording shall be made of hearings. These tape recordings shall be kept in the custody of the commission. The panel, the grievant, the respondent and or their University colleague(s) shall have reasonable access to these tapes during the processing of the grievance.

7. The presiding officer and the legal officer have the authority to obtain additional documents such as the dossiers of other members of the same department or faculty members in the same discipline in other parts of the University who recently or currently are alleged to have received more favorable treatment, provided that notice is given to those faculty members whose dossiers are to be examined. The panel may request the presiding officer to obtain expert opinion from inside or outside the University.

8. Since frank and candid evaluations are necessary to
aid appointment and promotion procedures, special care
must be taken in the examination of letters of recommendation and evaluation. Of course, both sides involved in
the grievance may stipulate, with the concurrence of
the legal officer, that such letters are irrelevant or
the grievant may already have had access to those documents by procedures unrelated to the filing of the
grievance. In such cases these questions will not
arise. In cases in which the presiding officer determines that information contained in letters of recommendation and evaluation concerning the grievant or
other members of the faculty is relevant, the panel,
to protect confidentiality and to further the broader
interests of the University, should consider, sep-
arately, the following issues:

    a. Did the department or other parties to the
decision make a reasonable effort to obtain
the views of experts not biased for or
against the grievant? In answering this
question, the presiding officer may let the
grievant examine and testify on a list of
names that includes but is not limited to
people who make the assessments; the panel
may also compare the letters obtained at
its behest, if any, with the original set.
    b. Did the requests for the views ask for
complete evaluations or did they imply
that a confirmation of a preexisting judgment was desired? In answering this
question, the panel may examine any written
requests for the views and may inquire of
the letter writers. Other methods may be
used at the discretion of the presiding
officer.
    c. Are the views, weighted by the reputa-
tions of the experts, when compared with
evaluations for others currently or recently
promoted, affirmative enough to occasion
concern that improper discrimination or
other grounds for grievance may have been
involved?
If the grievant is accompanied by a University
colleague who will have agreed to maintain
complete confidentiality with respect to all
information contained therein, the colleague

117

will be given access to the letters and
may question witnesses about the contents
of the letters. If the grievant does not
choose to be accompanied by a University
colleague, the letters shall not be dis-
closed; but the legal officer shall provide
to the grievant, to the greatest extent
feasible, an indication of the tenor of
the material in the letters so that he or
she may make such response as is possible
under the circumstances.

9. After the receipt of the panel's final report the
presiding officer shall return all borrowed documents
to their owners and turn over to the chair of the commission a complete file of the case--including a set of
documents, depositions, etc. and the tape recordings
of the hearings. The presiding officer shall destroy
all other materials. Except when the chair of the commission determines otherwise, the complete file shall
be destroyed three years after final action on the case
within the University. However, the panel report shall
be kept permanently on file.

ADDENDA TO THE FACULTY GRIEVANCE PROCEDURES

A Summary of the Procedures

The purpose of the new faculty grievance procedures,
like that of the former ones, is to provide a fair and
full peer review for faculty members who have a grievance.
The revisions are intended to accomplish this in ways
that will minimize the possibility of new conflicts and
injuries arising out of the implementation of the grievance procedures.
The essential features of the grievance procedures
as set out in Almanac on November 21, 1978 may be summarized as follows:

1. The administration of the grievance procedure
is the responsibility of a three-person Faculty
Grievance Commission composed of three members
of the standing faculty with the rank of full
professor. An independent legal officer is
to assist the commission in its work.

2. Preliminary procedures encourage the resolution of a complaint before the formal grievance procedures are invoked.

3. The grievance case is heard and decided by a hearing panel consisting of three faculty members. The panel is chosen at random from a list of 20 faculty members named by the Senate Advisory Committee and may be challenged.

4. The grievant may select a University colleague who normally will have academic qualifications in the grievant's field of study to provide expert assistance in the preparation and presentation of the case. If the grievant chooses to have a colleague, the respondent, who is appointed by the provost to act on behalf of the persons who made the decision complained of, may also have a nonadministrative colleague. It is not the intention to permit either party to have such a University colleague serve as legal advocate in the presentation of the case.

5. One of the members of the commission presides over the hearings. The legal officer prepares the case; this includes obtaining documents and setting the agenda for the hearings.

6. At the hearings each side may question witnesses introduced by the other side through the presiding officer. The role of the panel is largely that of a jury.

7. The panel presents its findings in a succinct report. If any element of the grievant's claim is upheld, the panel summarizes the salient facts that have led to its conclusions with respect to the injury done to the grievant. The report is sent to the grievant, the provost and the respondent.

8. The findings of the panel are not binding upon the provost. If the provost declines to implement a recommendation of

the panel his written communication to
the chair of the commission, the grievant
and the respondent shall include the detailed reasons, and shall be sent also to
the chairman of the Senate. The provost
may have complete access to the full documentation in the case.

9. Provisions are included for the recti-
fication of any administrative action or
practice that seemingly violates University
procedures or otherwise leads to inequitable
treatment.

10. All persons involved in a grievance
proceeding are enjoined to confidentialit-
and to the respect of the privacy of all
concerned.

11. Appeal is provided to the Senate
Committee on Academic Freedom and Responsibility in cases in which the provost
does not implement to the satisfaction
of the grievant a panel recommendation
involving reappointment, promotion or
tenure.

> --Committee on the Revision
> of Grievance Machinery
>
> Robert E. Davies (animal
>   biology)
> Larry Gross (communications)
> Irving B. Kravis (economics),
>   convener
> Philip G. Mechanick
>   (psychiatry)
> Covey Oliver (law)

Supplementary Understandings between the
Committee on the Revision of the Grievance
Machinery, Provost Eliot Stellar and Provost-
Elect Vartan Gregorian

1. It was agreed that the central administration
would bear the cost of released teaching time for members
of the new grievance commission up to one-quarter time.
Released teaching time, whether for one-quarter time or

more, is to be subject to request from the occupants of the posts and to review by the chairman of the Senate and the provost.

2. The independent legal officer should initially, at least, be a part-time person on a modest yearly retainer with arrangements for compensation at an hourly rate when actually employed. The chairman of the Senate and the provost should find a suitable person, if possible, for an initial three-year period.

3. With respect to the procedures part V:a, it is understood that the presiding officer may obtain expert opinion from inside or outside the University through a direct approach to such experts or through another faculty member or administrative officer, including the provost.

4. It is expected that the respondent will normally be a person who has been involved in the actions in the case.

5. It is, of course, understood that the provost may wish to take advice before designating the respondent.

APPENDIX C

CONFERENCE PARTICIPANTS

155 persons present, of whom 22 (14 percent) were men

Lynne S. Abel
Associate Dean
College of Arts and Sciences
Cornell University
Ithaca, New York 14853

Bette Adelman
Affirmative Action Officer
SUNY College at Geneseo
Geneseo, New York 11454

Marsha I. Altschuler
Postdoctoral Research Associate
Genetics and Development
Cornell University

B. Jean Apgar
Research Chemist
U.S. Nutrition Laboratory
Cornell University

Judith E. Aronson
Coordinator of Graduate Admissions
Cornell University

Leona Lynn Barsky
Graduate Student
Industrial and Labor Relations
Cornell University

Patricia A. BeGasse
Associate Professor
Broome Community College
Binghamton, New York 13905

Edna Berger
350 West 57 Street, #81
New York, New York 10019

Lois Black
Director of Affirmative Action
Syracuse University
Syracuse, New York 13210

Karen Bogart
Research Scientist
American Institutes for Research
1027 Riva Ridge Drive
Great Falls, Virginia 22066

Jean Bowering
Associate Professor
Department of Human Nutrition
Syracuse University
Syracuse, New York 13210

Leila A. Bradfield
8110 West ML Avenue
Kalamazoo, Michigan 49009

Wanda L. Brown
Chairwoman, Women Chemists Committee
American Chemical Society
212 Brightwood
San Antonio, Texas 78209

Mariam K. Chamberlain
Program Officer
Division of Education and Public Policy
Ford Foundation
320 E. 43 Street
New York, New York 10017

Appendix C

Marjorie Bell Chambers
Dean, The Union's Graduate School
Union for Experimenting Colleges and Universities
P.O. Box 85315
Cincinnati, Ohio 45201

Sarah J. Chilton
WVBR News
227 Linden Avenue
Ithaca, New York 14850

Kate Clancy
Nutritionist
Federal Trade Commission
Washington, D.C. 20580

Simone Clemhout
Associate Professor
Consumer Economics and Housing
Cornell University

Patricia L. Cohen
Class of 1982
Cornell Law School

John E. Coleman
Associate Professor
Classics
Cornell University

Charlotte W. Conable
Women's Studies Program and Policy Center
2025 Eye Street NW, Room 212
Washington, D.C. 20052

Jane Conable
10532 Alexander Road
Alexander, New York 14005

Marta J. Concha
Graduate Student
Genetics and Development
Cornell University

Alice H. Cook
Professor Emerita
School of Industrial and Labor Relations
Cornell University

Catherine P. Cook
1660 Mecklenburg Road
Ithaca, New York 14850

Nancy Costlow
Graduate Student
Biochemistry
Cornell University

Jane D. Crawford
Health Careers Coordinator and
 Associate Director, Career Center
Cornell University

Ruth W. Darling
111 Midway Road
Ithaca, New York 14850

Helen C. Davies
Associate Professor
Microbiology, School of Medicine
University of Pennsylvania
Philadelphia, Pennsylvania 19104

Robert E. Davies
Benjamin Franklin Professor of Molecular Biology
 and University Professor, School of Medicine
University of Pennsylvania
Philadelphia, Pennsylvania 19104

Edwina Devereux
142 Hawthorne Place
Ithaca, New York 14850

Alice Diamond
Graduate Student
Industrial and Labor Relations
Cornell University

Appendix C

Marjorie V. Dibble
Chairperson, Department of Human Nutrition
Syracuse University
Syracuse, New York 13210

Amy S. Doherty
Syracuse University Archivist
E. S. Bird Library
Syracuse, New York 13210

Marjorie F. Doris, M.D.
Gannett Health Center
Cornell University

Peg Downey
Assistant Director for Program Development
American Association of University Women
2401 Virginia Avenue NW
Washington, D.C. 20037

Nancy Du Boise
Class of 1982
School of Industrial and Labor Relations
Cornell University

Rada Dyson-Hudson
Associate Professor
Anthropology
Cornell University

Elizabeth Earle
Associate Professor
Plant Breeding and Biometry
Cornell University

Shirley K. Egan
Associate University Counsel
Cornell University

Jennie Farley
Assistant Professor
School of Industrial and Labor Relations
Cornell University

Charlotte J. Farris
Director, Project MOVE
SUNY College of Technology at Utica
Utica, New York   13502

Sarah Fast
Graduate Student
Natural Resources
Cornell University

Harold Feldman
Professor
Human Development and Family Studies
Cornell University

Margaret Feldman
Professor
Psychology
Ithaca College
Ithaca, New York   14850

June M. Fessenden-Raden
Associate Professor
Biochemistry and Biology and Society
Cornell University

Steven Fisher
Class of 1981
College of Arts and Sciences
Cornell University

J. Anthony Gaenslen
1571 Slaterville Road
Ithaca, New York   14850

Mary L. Gangl
Graduate Student
Counseling and Human Resources
SUNY College at Buffalo
Buffalo, New York   14222

Sarah E. Garlan
Class of 1981
College of Arts and Sciences
Cornell University

Appendix C

Kenneth I. Greisen
Professor, Physics
Dean of the Faculty
Cornell University

Peggy Haine
Assistant Director
Sponsored Programs
Cornell University

Tove Helland Hammer
Assistant Professor
School of Industrial and Labor Relations
Cornell University

Rita W. Harris
Director of Personnel
Veterinary Medicine
Cornell University

Louise Hayes
Class of 1983
College of Arts and Sciences
Cornell University

Susan Hellerman
Class of 1981
College of Arts and Sciences
Cornell University

David W. Henderson
Associate Professor
Mathematics
Cornell University

Francine Herman
Associate Professor
Hotel Administration
Cornell University

Darlene L. Hillery
Class of 1981
School of Industrial and Labor Relations
Member, Board of Trustees
Cornell University

Antonia Glasse
AAUW Postdoctoral Fellow
320 University Avenue
Ithaca, New York 14850

Diane Gnagnarelli
Class of 1981
Human Ecology
Cornell University

Elenor Gnagarelli
1115 Park Street
Syracuse, New York 13208

Rose K. Goldsen
Professor
Sociology
Cornell University

Sharon Gonsalves, Intern
New York State Education Department
Occupational Education Special Programs
Room 1610, Twin Towers
99 Washington Avenue
Albany, New York 12230

A. Elizabeth Gordon
Research Associate
Entomology
Cornell University

Lois S. Gray
Professor and Associate Dean
Division of Extension and Public Service
School of Industrial and Labor Relations
Cornell University

Patricia McAfee Green
Reed Library
SUNY College at Fredonia
Fredonia, New York 14063

Helen Greisen
Research Associate
Veterinary Medicine
Cornell University

Appendix C

Mariana W. Hitchner
Route 1, Box K-54
Worton, Maryland 21678

David M. Hoffman
Graduate Student
Chemistry
Cornell University

Katherine Albro Houpt
Assistant Professor of Physiology
Veterinary Medicine
Cornell University

Helen Howard
College for Human Development
Syracuse University
Syracuse, New York 13210

Silvia Huber
Assistant to the President for
 Affirmative Action
SUNY College at Binghamton
Binghamton, New York 13901

Laura Foster Huenneke
Graduate Student
Ecology and Systematics
Cornell University

Carolyn Ingalls
Lecturer in Business
SUNY College at Oneonta
Oneonta, New York 13820

Anastasia K. Johnson
Assistant to the Chair
Department of Sociology
SUNY College at Buffalo
Buffalo, New York 14222
 Representing Affirmative Action Committee
 United University Professions

Mary Ann C. Keenan
1301 Euclid Avenue
Syracuse, New York 13224

Marian Kennedy
Assistant Professor
School of Industrial and Labor Relations
Cornell University

Peter Kingsley
Postdoctoral Fellow
Nutritional Sciences
Cornell University

Marian M. Kira
Affirmative Action Program Coordinator for
 Cooperative Extension
Cornell University

Patricia Klein
Assistant Professor
Social Science Department
College of General Studies
Western Michigan University
Kalamazoo, Michigan 49008

David Kline
Graduate Student
Physics
Cornell University

Nancy Lampen
Assistant Professor
Monroe Community College
Rochester, New York 14623

Alicia Lawless
Class of 1984
Industrial and Labor Relations
Cornell University

Judith Long Laws
Associate Professor
Sociology
Syracuse University
Syracuse, New York 13210

Lee C. Lee
Associate Professor
Human Development and Family Studies
Cornell University

131

Appendix C

Jacqueline Livingston
Former Assistant Professor
Photography
Cornell University

Jean Locey
Assistant Professor
Art
Cornell University

Bernice B. MacDonald
Equity Coordinator
New Jersey Division, AAUW
10 Cypress Avenue
North Caldwell, New Jersey   07006

Dorothy C. Manning
College Librarian
Keuka College
Keuka Park, New York   14478

Julie T. Mellor
Graduate Student
Industrial and Labor Relations
Cornell University

Nancy S. Meltzer
Assistant Dean
College of Human Ecology
Cornell University

Virginia Merriam
Visiting Professor
Genetics and Development
Cornell University

Jeannette Miccinati
Assistant Professor
SUNY College at Buffalo
Buffalo, New York   14222

Carolyn Miller
Monroe Community College
Rochester, New York   14623

Frank B. Miller
Professor
School of Industrial and Labor Relations
Cornell University

Peggy M. Miller
Assistant Professor of Management
Keuka College
Keuka Park, New York 14478

Nell Mondy
Associate Professor
Nutritional Sciences
Cornell University

Michael J. Montgomery
Director
Office of Equal Opportunity
Cornell University

Burrell E. Montz
Assistant Professor
Geography
SUNY College at Binghamton
Binghamton, New York 13901

Ellen Morris
Assistant Professor
Architecture
Cornell University

Gordon L. Myers
Director of Personnel and Affirmative Action
SUNY College at Canton
Canton, New York 13617

Debra Nero
Graduate Student
Genetics and Development
Cornell University

Ray T. Oglesby
Professor
Natural Resources
Cornell University

Christian F. Otto
Associate Professor
Architecture
Cornell University

Robert J. Pasciullo
Visiting Professor
School of Industrial and Labor Relations
Cornell University

Jean G. Pearson
Administrative Manager
Social Science Systems Analysis
Cornell University

Erica G. Polakoff
Graduate Student
Education
Cornell University

Marcia S. Pottle
Research Support Specialist
Chemistry
Cornell University

Marion Potts
Professor
Human Development and Family Studies
Cornell University

Susan E. Prensky
Class of 1981
College of Arts and Sciences
Cornell University

Dorothy M. Proud
Professor Emerita
Human Ecology
Cornell University
5107 24th Avenue NE, Apt. 17
Seattle, Washington 98105

Laura M. Purdy
Assistant Professor
Philosophy
Wells College
Aurora, New York 13026

Joanna Rankin
Assistant Professor
Physics
University of Vermont
Burlington, Vermont   05401

Karen Kaufmann Richards
Graduate Student
History
Cornell University

Barbara Richardson
Research Associate
Social Processes/Women's Research Team
National Institute of Education
1200 19th and M Street
Washington, D.C.   20208

Robert F. Risley
Professor
School of Industrial and Labor Relations
Cornell University

Gennifer F. Rommel
Class of 1982
School of Industrial and Labor Relations
Cornell University

Ann F. Roscoe
Coordinator, Title IX Committee and Provost's
 Advisory Committee on the Status of Women
Office of Equal Opportunity
Cornell University

Joseph L. Rossen
Professor and Associate Director
School of Electrical Engineering
Cornell University

Mary P. Rowe
Special Assistant to the President
Massachusetts Institute of Technology
Cambridge, Massachusetts   02139

Appendix C

Anne J. Russ
Director of Career Planning
Wells College
Aurora, New York   13026

Bernice R. Sandler
Director, Project on the Status and Education
 of Women
Association of American Colleges
1818 R Street
Washington, D.C.   20009

Mary E. Schum
Affirmative Action Officer
Broome Community College
Binghamton, New York   13905

Ruth Schwartz
Professor
Nutritional Sciences
Cornell University

Marilyn F. Semrau
Assistant Professor
Mathematics
Monroe Community College
Rochester, New York   14623

Susan P. Shrader
Assistant Professor
Mathematics
Monroe Community College
Rochester, New York   14623

A. Helen Smith
Vice President for Affirmative Action
SUNY College at Delhi
Delhi, New York   13753

Janet Smith-Kintner
Assistant Director
Learning Skills Center, Office of Minority
 Educational Affairs (COSEP)
Instructor, Physics
Cornell University

136

Marcia J. Spaeth
Associate Dean of Professional Studies
SUNY College at Cortland
Cortland, New York 13045

Adrian M. Srb
Jacob Gould Schurman Professor
Genetics and Development
Cornell University

Jozetta H. Srb
Research Associate
School of Industrial and Labor Relations
Cornell University

Claudia Stallman
Department of Geography
SUNY College at Binghamton
Binghamton, New York 13901

Ruth E. Stark
Assistant Professor
Chemistry
Amherst College
Amherst, Massachusetts 01002

Peter C. Stein
Professor
Physics
Cornell University

B. Joyce Stephens
Associate Professor
Sociology
SUNY College at Fredonia
Fredonia, New York 14063

Daniel N. Tapper
Professor
Veterinary Medicine
Cornell University

Christine Tarrant
Graduate Student
Entomology
Cornell University

Appendix C

Glenna I. Thaler
Assistant Executive Director
Cornell University Council
Cornell University

Constance H. Timberlake
Chairperson, Community Services
College for Human Development
Syracuse University
Syracuse, New York 13210

Bob Topor
Assistant Director
Media Services
Cornell University

Martha A. Turnbull
Director of Personnel
Ithaca College
Ithaca, New York 14850

Judith P. Vladeck
Vladeck, Elias, Vladeck & Engelhard, P.C.,
 Counsellors at Law
1501 Broadway
New York, New York 10036

Louise D. Walsh
Graduate Student
Industrial and Labor Relations
Cornell University

Carolyn B. Ware
Assistant Vice President for Academic Affairs
SUNY College at Binghamton
Binghamton, New York 13901

Barbara Mayer Wertheimer
Associate Professor
School of Industrial and Labor Relations
New York City
Cornell University

Beverly Henderson West
Lecturer
Mathematics
Cornell University

Jeanne A. White
Associate Librarian
Albert R. Mann Library
Cornell University

Antoinette M. Wilkinson
Senior Lecturer
Communication Arts
Cornell University

Ruth L. Wynn
Associate Professor
Child and Family Studies
Syracuse University
Syracuse, New York 13210

Elizabeth Bixler Yanof
DeWitt Building
Ithaca, New York 14850

Carol Day Young
Graduate Student
Education
Cornell University

Judith T. Younger
Professor
Cornell Law School

Donna M. Zahorik
Former Assistant Professor, Psychology,
 Cornell University
105 Cobb Street
Ithaca, New York 14850

Alton W. Zanders
Affirmative Action Office
SUNY College of Environmental Science and Forestry
Syracuse, New York 13210

EDUCATIONAL INSTITUTIONS REPRESENTED

Amherst College
Broome Community College

Appendix C

Cornell University
George Washington University
Ithaca College
Keuka College
Loyola-Marymount, Los Angeles
Monroe Community College
Princeton University
SUNY College at Binghamton
SUNY College at Buffalo
SUNY College at Canton
SUNY College at Cortland
SUNY College at Delhi
SUNY College at Fredonia
SUNY College at Geneseo
SUNY College at Oneonta
SUNY College at Syracuse
SUNY College at Utica
Syracuse University
University of Pennsylvania
University of Vermont
Wells College
Western Michigan University

STATES REPRESENTED

District of Columbia
Massachusetts
Michigan
New Jersey
New York
Ohio
Pennsylvania
Texas
Virginia
Vermont
Washington

OTHER ORGANIZATIONS REPRESENTED

American Association of University Women, national office
American Association of University Women, New Jersey Division
American Chemical Society, Women Chemists Committee
American Institutes for Research

Participants

Association of American Colleges
Federal Trade Commission
Ford Foundation
National Institute of Education
United University Professions, Inc.

141

APPENDIX D

CONTRIBUTORS

Helen C. Davies is associate professor of
microbiology, School of Medicine, University of
Pennsylvania, where she has served as a researcher
and teacher for thirty years. Davies earned the A.B.
in chemistry at Brooklyn College (1944), the M.S. in
biochemistry at the University of Rochester (1950),
and the Ph.D. in biochemistry from the University of
Pennsylvania (1960). She has undertaken research on
the chemistry, immunology, and mechanism of action of
the streptococcal M proteins and on the reactions of
Cytochrome c, Cytochrome Oxidase, and Cytochrome c
reductase in electron transport. She has also undertaken research on the recruitment and retention of
minority group members and women in biomedical careers.
Davies has been elected to many faculty committees
associated with faculty self-governance, review procedures, and the status of women and minorities. She
won awards for excellence in teaching in 1971, 1977,
and 1979.

Robert E. Davies in Benjamin Franklin Professor
of Molecular Biology and University Professor, School
of Medicine, University of Pennsylvania, where he has
served as a member of the faculty since 1955. Davies
earned the B.Sc. with First Class Honours in chemistry
at the University of Manchester (1941), the M.Sc. by
thesis there (1942), and the Ph.D. by thesis (1949)
at the University of Sheffield. Davies also holds
the M.A. by decree from Oxford University (1956) and
has been a fellow of the Royal Society, London, since
1966. In 1977, Davies was elected honorary life member

of the New York Academy of Sciences in recognition of
his contribution to science. He has been author
or coauthor of some 230 papers in his specialty,
edited journals in his field, and served on numerous
university committees, most recently as chairman of
the University Senate Committee on Academic Freedom
and Responsibility (1978–79 and 1980–81).

Jennie Farley is assistant professor in the New
York State School of Industrial and Labor Relations at
Cornell University. Farley holds three degrees from
Cornell: the B.A. in English (1954), the M.S. in
development sociology (1969), and the Ph.D. in
sociology and communications (1970). She was cofounder
of Cornell's Women's Studies Program in 1970 and served
as its first director from 1972 to 1976. Author of
journal articles in some fifteen professional journals,
Farley is also author of Affirmative Action and the
Woman Worker: Guidelines for Personnel Management, a
handbook for personnel practitioners published by
American Management Associations in 1979.

Mary P. Rowe has been special assistant to the
president of the Massachusetts Institute of Technology
since 1973. She earned the B.A. in history and international relations at Swarthmore College (1957) and
the Ph.D. in economics at Columbia University (1971).
Rowe serves as ombudswoman at MIT where she is also
involved in the review of work structures and processes,
teaching, research, and writing. Rowe serves as consultant to corporations and nonprofit institutions
concerned with local, national, and international problems of work process including nonunion grievance procedures, mentorship systems, child care, state-organ-
ized employment and training programs, and scientific
education and training. Rowe has served as director of
a Carnegie Corporation-funded project at Radcliffe Institute, where she designed a release-time program for
faculty and an internship program for students to benefit senior women faculty and women students. She has
also directed an OEO-funded project at Harvard University concerned with child care demand and undertaken
consulting on black business ownership in Boston. Rowe
supervised a field work project with 170 Nigerian in-
dustrialists between 1963 and 1966.

Bernice R. Sandler is currently executive associate
with the Association of American Colleges, Washington,
D.C., where she has served as director of the Project
on the Status and Education of Women since 1971. Before
that, she served as deputy director of the Women's
Action Program at HEW, a project set up to evaluate the
impact on women of HEW programs. Sandler holds a degree
in counseling and personnel services from the University
of Maryland, where she has served as visiting lecturer.
She has also taught psychology at Mt. Vernon College and
has been a psychologist at HEW, research assistant, nurs-
ery school teacher, employment counselor, adult education
instructor, and, like many women, a secretary. Sandler
holds four honorary doctorates; she was the recipient
in 1974 of the Athena Award given by the Intercollegiate
Association of Women Students, the 1976 Elizabeth Boyer
Award given by the Women's Equity Action League (WEAL),
and cowinner in 1976 of a Rockefeller Public Service
Award from Princeton University. Author of more than
thirty articles on sex discrimination in higher education,
Sandler has testified before numerous congressional committees on that subject. As former head of the Action
Committee for Federal Contract Compliance of the Women's
Equity Action League, Sandler filed formal charges of sex
discrimination against some 250 universities and colleges.

Judith P. Vladeck is an attorney with Vladeck, Elias,
Vladeck & Engelhard, New York City. She has served as an
adjunct member of the faculty of the New York State School
of Industrial and Labor Relations, Cornell University, in
the metropolitan district branch in New York City. A
member of the New York bar, Vladeck is coauthor (with
attorney Margaret M. Young) of "Sex Discrimination: It's
Not Academic" (Women's Rights Law Reporter, 1978) and coauthor (with attorney Stephen C. Vladeck) of "Collective
Bargaining in Higher Education" (PLI, 1975). She earned
the bachelor's degree at Hunter College (1945) and
the LL.B. from Columbia (1947). A longtime board member
of the New York Civil Liberties Union, Vladeck has served
as cooperating attorney with the Workers' Defense League.
Her specialty is representing unions in the private and
public sector on behalf of plaintiffs. Vladeck has also
represented plaintiffs alleging sex discrimination in
employment practices in universities.

Index

AAUP, 48, 50
AAUW, 72, 75, 76
Abel, J., 46
ACLU, 75
Adelman, Bette, 93-94
Aetna Life and Casualty
  Foundation, viii
Affirmative action, ix,
  66, 70, 88, 91
Alexander v. Gardner-
  Denver, 21
Altrusa, 75
American Psychological
  Association, 78
Amherst College, 92
Arbitration, 16, 19-21, 59
Armstrong, Ann, 82
Association for Women in
  Science (AWIS), 50
Astin, H. S., 38
Authorship, concealing
  sex in, 57

Bendix Corporation, 30
Berkeley. See California,
  University of, at Berkeley
Bird, C., 36
Brown University, viii, 17,
  55, 91, 101
Brown, Wanda L., 97-98
Business and Professional
  Women's Clubs, 76

California State Legis-
  lature, 71
California, University of, at
  Berkeley, vii, 34, 58
California, University of,
  at San Jose, 58
Chemistry, women in, 35, 97
Chicago, University of,
  34, 87
Childers, K., 45
Citation analysis, 42-44,
  56-57
City University of New
  York (CUNY), vii, 7, 9,
  12, 14, 18
Coalitions, politics of,
  76-77, 86
Conarroe, J., 46
Confidentiality, 11, 99
Cook, Alice, 73
Cooperating organizations,
  as sponsors of conference,
  viii-ix
Cornell Eleven, vii, viii,
  9, 12, 13
Cornell University, vii,
  13, 88, 95, 96-97, 98, 101
Cunningham, Mary, 30-31

Davies, Helen C., x, 34-65,
  67, 73, 85, 94
Davies, Robert E., x, 34-65,
  100

145

Index